CONFESSIONS

OF A FAILED

EGOIST

AND OTHER ESSAYS

TREVOR BLAKE

UNDERWORLD AMUSEMENTS

Designed and prepared by Kevin I. Slaughter
for Underworld Amusements.
www.UnderworldAmusements.com

Cover illustration by Josh Latta.
www.LattaLand.com

First Edition
ISBN13: 978-0-9885536-5-1

Originally published in OVO,
here corrected and expanded:
    "Trajectory Through Anarchism." June 2010.
    "So You Want to Meet an Alien?" July 2010.
    "Yes You Can Say No." September 2010.
    "Co-Remoting with the Thunderous." November 2010.
    "Multiple Name Identities." December 2010.
    "My Crowded Fist Theater Shouting Fire..." August 2012.
    "Why Should I Speak of Them?" November 2012.

The author thanks tENTATIVELY, a cONVENIENCE
for technical assistance on "Co-Remoting with the
Thunderous."

TABLE OF CONTENTS

TREVOR BLAKE

CONFESSIONS OF A FAILED EGOIST

I

I am an egoist, a circular thinker of the most self-contained philosophy. Keep reading, though, and you'll see I'm not a very good Unique One. I see rusty rivets and loose lashings in the *HMS Egoism*. Egoism is the contrarian's philosophy, and so of course I begin this book with a broadside against it.

Egoism is the claim that the individual is the measure of all things. In ethics, in epistemology, in aesthetics, in society, the Individual is the best and only arbitrator. Egoism claims social convention, laws, other people, religion, language, time and all other forces outside of the Individual are an impediment to the liberty and existence of the Individual. Such impediments may be tolerated but they have no special standing to the Individual, who may elect to ignore or subvert or destroy them as He can. In egoism the State has no monopoly to take tax or to wage war.

A few words about words. Max Stirner called the individual *der einzige* (the Unique One) in his 1845 book *Der Einzige und sein Eigentum*. 'Individual' and 'unique one' didn't have that legitimacy loaned by Latin lexicalization, and so the book was popularized as *The*

Ego and His Own in the same way that Freud's simple *das Ich* (I) was duded up as 'the ego.' I am *the* subject matter, the proper noun, while y'all are objects. Thus I, Me and Mine are all quite capital. Most of the time we have our faces buried in smartphone simulacra, maps and not territories. But when I speak of egoism, I speak of egoism with gnostic directness and not the idea of egoism or egoism-in-itself.

I know how this sounds. This book doesn't make sense. The excessive word play is aggravating. Much of it is crazy talk. Too much repetition. The amount of background knowledge in high and low culture required to get the joke much less the point is unreasonable. Sir, *there is no other means of expressing egoism.* I can only give you a rope, a snake, four trees, a wall and two curtains. It's up to you to make your own egoist elephant. Try reading it aloud, one chapter at a time, or just buy copies for your friends and forget about it.

Now... let's strap this unhealthy specimen to the dissection table and get to work. Egoism is refuted by the simple existence of bodies and the complex matter of minds. Egoism doesn't hold water socially or philosophically. But as the contrarian's philosophy, disproof is not enough to make egoism go poof. The magician's cape whirls once again to reveal egoism puts the imp in impossible.

II

You're too young to remember this, but at one time you... weren't. Your mammy and your pappy did the deed, sperm met egg and at some point after that you... were. Egoism must account for when you got your *you* on. It seems silly to suggest I was before I was, so I likely wasn't before conception. I hung out as an unviable fetus for months, and there's no standing on your own two feet when you're hanging upside down in someone else's womb. Plenty of babies are born early or late and require intervention by others to survive. I was not born with anything close to agency over My actions, and was a floppy poopy mess for who knows how long. With self-control of My body came My first blurts of language, a skill I hope to develop to adequacy some day. The human brain does not stop developing until after the teenage years. That's a good double decade of uncertainty as to when the ego enters the me-arena. Egoism has the problem of being unable to define when the Unique One comes into being and thus in saying who is and is not (yet) an Individual. This is true even when the egoist is asking when He, Himself, became an Individual. Egoism talks about the Individual, but who that individual is cannot be talked about. The stages of acquiring individual status I listed above are just the most likely dates I started me-ing. Perhaps it was the first time I stood up and walked, or broke a heart, or paid all My own bills, or registered for the draft.

　　Whatever ragged race you're running, I assure you the finish line looms and is shared by the One and all. Death is certain but dying is a puzzle for egoists. Egoism has the problem of being unable to define when the Unique One ceases to be and thus in saying who is or was an individual. Egoism talks about the Individual, but who that individual is cannot be talked about. The postponement of death through medical means, the possibility of transhuman life extension, of cryogenics, muddies the waters of ego death. How much or in what ways I die the death before I'm good and gone I cannot say. Come visit me in Valhalla and I'll tell you what I've learned.

The most egregious elements of childhood are elevated and enshrined in egoism. The lack of ability or interest in differentiating the self from the environment, the temper tantrums, the selfishness, the exaggerated emphasis on rules followed and broken—send that sprog to the 'splainin' room for a sound spanking!

Egoism not only has the problem of being unable to define when any particular Individual appears, but also when any Individual at all first appeared. Egoism cannot say whether there were egoist Neanderthals, or before them egoist possum-critters who stole dinosaur eggs, or perhaps egoist dinosaurs, or egoist fish, egoist algae... don't stop at selfish genes when you can imagine selfish molecules. There is likely a line of before and after egoism emerged in evolution. Egoism cannot say where that line is drawn. Egoism can scoop the idea of animal rights out of the litter box as easily as any other idea of natural rights. But the idea of animal egos, the Unique One of non-human animals, is snarling and snapping and ready to engage any thinker trying cage it.

Being alone is a crowded place. Human DNA is measurably made up of ancient viruses. Every human cell is also the home of mitochondria. A person is more like a park of microbiomes. As much as I feel like myself, I'm more of a siphonophore. This gives "we're number one!" a whole new meaningless meaning.

This book is the world's burden somewhere in between the any-day-now dawn of artificial intelligence in the 1950s and the supercontext. The Internet is enough of a person for many people most of the time. It's past time for humanity to clean himself up because eventually we will have someone else to talk to. And that someone else may be far more of a Unique One than any human could ever be. A crafty artificial intelligence might scan and upload you into a simulation without your being aware of the change, initiating even further erosion to the foundations of egoism. Then transhumanism won't seem so dry and we can have a little sin in our singularity.

I once flew free from the web of words. Then came speech, and literacy, and forever after that which is Me is known and expressed in that which is not Me. Language is inherently social and the social is inherently outside of Me. It doesn't entertain My ego to think pre-linguistic babies are alone themselves. The dead and the incommunicative are also not egoistic. Language makes none of us egoists, and that all of us are not egoists means double trouble for the idea of the Unique One.

I am My body, and I am the Unique One. At the same time every few weeks I shave My head and My body carves off bits of what was Me. Where that one-of-a-kind ego is when the body can divide is a mystery. Egoism has the problem of being unable to define where in the body, or in how much of the body, the Individual exists. Egoism talks about the Individual, but who that individual is cannot be talked about. Compound that mystery by the body's requirements for nutritious food, water, air, physical exercise and the sex. That's some kind of weak-ass id that can only be bothered to be by the intake of the other.

I am the only egoist in history, or maybe just the best. There doesn't seem to be a logical alternative. The ego being unbound by logic, I note a handful of other I's out there. How there can be more than one Unique One is above My pay grade. Egoism has the problem of being a philosophy for the Individual in a world where more than one individual exists. This problem is compounded by competition between Individuals, the resolution for which egoism has no solution.

Some egoists claim that "nature's law is tooth and claw," that there is a natural right and the prone bodies of the vanquished point to those who possess it. But isn't it convenient that title holders of natural rights are only known after the final bell? Might is the law of all life, yet some groups are more might than others. Every individual must struggle for existence, yet that ghost of might-right inside them takes a vacation once in a while and eventually moves away to stay. What good to me is a natural right that I can't know about until after I've used it, and which may leave me when I need it most, and which someone else might have more of than me? *Lex talionis* is the projection of matter-of-fact outcomes of conflict onto a cave wall and calling that lack of light a natural right. To the victor goes the spoil—sure, but no need to get all wheely about it. "The mighty win" is true but it is a mistake to say "the mighty ought to win." Evolution is the failure of the non-adaptive to survive, not the survival of the fittest. The former is how things seem to be, the later is the mistake of intelligent design. The philosophy of might making right slips into spookiness on two counts. First, to say that the outcome of a conflict makes the best of all possible worlds as evidence by its existence is a just-so tale. Worse, it is of no use to Me. All that was is not what is, and brother I is. It might be that might was right, but I have no right to be bothered by that that. Second, were I to adjust the adverbs and announce might is right, that the mighty should prevail and the vanquished should wail their woe, I set above myself a should I must serve or submit to—a substitute for myself. Not only is might is right a mistake, but kind of whiney, too. "But I was supposed to win... whaaa..." Egoism is made of sterner stuff.

III

Because the body boundary is blurred the temptation is to say that the ego is the mind. The ego becomes a ghost of the gaps, and as soon as we chase it from one hidey-hole it finds another.

I'm here to tell you that consciousness is a physical process. Placing the ego in the mind rather than the body is like placing a man in New York City and saying he's not in New York State. We have a word for the soul that sounds secular—mind—but naming a thing does not make it so. I am out of My mind. I have a brain and I suspect it is largely like yours. The brain is not a point without weight or mass, as the mindless mind is supposed to be. The mind is to the body as a shadow is to light. The mysterious magical mind is a singularity. It is a phantom captain that is the real you. Evidence enough for me that for all the sizzle in the steak, we're made of meat.

A knock to the noggin can bruise a brain and from that can come a change in consciousness. Egoism has the problem of being unable to place the ego in a mind without a body. The same difficulties of locating egoism in the body show up when brain injuries reveal the mind is a function of the body.

No need to be brained to get physical with your

thinky parts. You've probably been to sleep recently. The idea of a crystalline emission-dot of identity is done in by dreams and dissolved in slumber. Mind goes bye-bye right quick in sleep, while the brain does what comes naturally. Egoism has the problem of explaining where the ego goes when the body is asleep. The agency and the singularity of the ego is not evident in a person who is asleep. Turn off your mind, relax and float downstream.

I withhold My fealty to any baron of the brain, any ur-me that is above Myself. There is a Me that could smoke a fine cigar more often, a Me that grows less healthy for it, and a Me that budgets the money to groceries and not cigars. I do not claim My most recent action or thought, or the one I feel or think the strongest, is the real Me. I have no need for a me and a real me (and a really real me, and a really really real me, etc.). Just Me. Egoism has the problem of who that Me might be.

Don't get me started on mental illness. Well, okay. A case of the crazies is bound to jump in any review of the wrongs of egoism. More than one and more than two eminent egoists have been unable to care for themselves in adulthood and lost all the beauty in their life (my delineators for minimal mental malady). There are at least fifty shades to this portrait of Dorian Grey. Egoism has the problem of explaining Individuals who are not individuals. Those species of insanity that hear voices knock a hole in the walls of Castle Ego. They are one-in-many, something the ego is supposed to depose yet there she blows. States of self-harm likewise mock notions of egos as agents acting on self-interest. Some individuals have obsessions and urges they cannot control and do not want, and egoism must answer the question of who is the Unique One in a person of two minds. Some people have broken the shackles of constricting rationality such that they are free to be entirely unable to communicate or make deliberate body motions, either due to being comatose or having life-long and constant violent spasms. Egoism as an affectation of the college educated is all well and good, but what it might have to say of those at the lowest end of the IQ spectrum is unclear. Egoism's offer to the differently-saned promises too much and not nearly enough.

Don't discriminate against the dicephalic. Plenty of people are plurals. They used to urge you to step right up and see the Siamese twins. Today the term of choice is co-joined. One body with two brains throws everything the West knows about the Self into seething turmoil. As the ideology of Identity, egoism most of all must muster a multi-brained bromide in reply to these outliers. Abigail and Brittany Hensel await egoism's answer.

Evolution more blind than love blessed our bodies with cheat codes. A few small ounces of fluids including that master molecule caffeine and hey, where'd I go? I seem to be a happier person, glib and gabby and ready to write egoist essays all the live-long day. Alcohol also tosses the Self-script and goes improv. Drugs confirm consciousness is a chemical condition, offering ongoing opportunities to ask where you at. Drugs that have strong and predictable influence on the Self are a challenge to the selfish philosophy. As drugs complete the Self but exist outside the Self, there is confusion as to where the Self is located.

Men and women's brains are similar but not the same. Everybody knows it, but that fashionable spook of temperance—I mean suffrage—I mean feminism—keeps many men mum to please madam. Women tell me their bodies have patterns Mine sure doesn't, depending on if they are babied up or not. Ask your local intersex egoist about the vast difference in egos by sex. I will merely note that it is, and where there is two there can be no One.

IV

Time! Now there's a problem for egoism. Befores and afters can squat where they sat, but right now there's a right now that won't sit still for the camera. My consciousness at any particular now is already in the past. The now of Me looking at a beautiful woman or having My thumb slammed in a door sure seem different lengths of sequential instantaneous. I doubt My brain has a gravity field to bend time so the moment of ego seems hard to handle. I see star light in a now that happened long ago and right this second. There's a lag between thought and motion, between perception and awareness of perception. Egoism has to punch in on the time question.

Solipsism slips in the egoist envelope. Solipsism is on board with the Unique One, going further to say that all else is a projection of that the One. Egoism is okay with others existing, just not in elevating them above the Self. But who that Self is, and how there can be more than one One, and why might it be that others aren't just imagined, for these egoism is left shrugging.

Egoism fails to scale. The physical laws that are solid enough to run the universe seem to break down when you look at the smallest components of the universe. What we mean when we talk about individuals is clear enough, but where and who that Individual might be is far from clear.

Finally, egoism can't be true because egoism can't be true. Nobody really thinks like this and certainly nobody really acts like this. There is enough to go around for everybody, we just need to teach each other to be nicer. I am a fit judge to know I am not a fit judge in what I am am not a fit judge to be. The way out of the prisoner's dilemma is to stay a prisoner.

Individuality may be a passing fancy after all. What I think of as an I likely didn't exist in pre-history. For most of human history only royalty were sovereign, with most of the rest being interchangeable and anonymous. Christianity might not have had a single word to say about the immorality of keeping slaves, but it did invent the notion that even (male) slaves had souls that could go to heaven. Feudalism and caste societies offered up perhaps a dozen types of individual, but no more. The modern conceit of democracy, that every vote counts, that having an identity card and being fingerprinted makes you a special snowflake, might turn out to have been one more form of 19th Century madness that flamed bright and died out.

V

For all the thunder and lightning that storms around self-centered egoism, it seems the field is muddied where impregnable citadel walls were supposed to stand. The I overlaps into others (hi mom & dad), exists in inherently social language, is born and dies in a body that can get boogered up and needs must eat, is blasted through time and runs the risk of putting an -ism in front of the ego.

This is crazy talk, but it is not *just* crazy talk. If you ask Me, in for a penny is in for a pounding.

All systems say they will set you free if you becomes one of us. A wormy bait but a switch so successful it swallows societies. I don't know what egoism offers you, but I can tell you how it's worked out for me. Pretty good, My friend.

My confessions reveal why egoism cannot be true and is not internally consistent. Truth and consistency to an egoist are clever tools, yes, but never are they His master. There is no disproof of egoism. I've conveyed egoism and I've conveyed how I live My life, but not where those aren't the same thing (egoism being the most tempting not-me to serve of all, but it goes away just hungry!). It is plain you have to draw the line somewhere, and my point of interest is Myself.

Egoism is a philosophy for men, and I'm a card-carrying member (or am I a member-carrying card?). I am profoundly disengaged from the process of deciding who should or shouldn't be an egoist. There have been and are and likely will be women egoists. I also say the rough-and-tumble tone of egoism puts a smile on the face of more men and a scowl on the face of more women. Women might be for or against force and philosophy in the world, but it's going to be men who carry it out and have it carried out against them. I have My just-so stories about why that might be, but they aren't very interesting or surprising stories.

Egoism is the funniest philosophy. Funny ha-ha and funny strange. No other ethic is as wealthy in wordplay or is as full of pratfalls. No other philosophy is as deeply entwined with its own counter-arguments. Egoism is closer to poetry than propaganda, reminding you of something rather than hitting you on the head with it. Nihilism is the confused notion that nothing matters but it should, a mistake not repeated by egoism. To paraphrase some wag, I will bear My blindness and ruin with laughter, I will die laughing.

The question (as in the singular question) of Western philosophy is that of identity. What a thing is, how one thing can become another thing, how a thing can move and the like. Eastern philosophy also considered the individual, then said 'no thank you.' There is an unbroken line from Plato's theory of Forms to atomic theory to egoism, and I'm going to ride that line all the way to the terminal. The world turned on its head in the late 19th/early 20th Century and I'm a fan of the acrobatics. The Western way of literature is littered with alliteration, a tradition that goes back to Beowolf. If you are a reader of English and a thinker of the modern age, you need to know about egoism (not that egoism needs to know about you).

Politics, philosophy, ethics, all those thinky things, can be corralled into two camps. One is the prescriptive, which tell you what to do. One is the descriptive, which tell you what happened. Egoism is an exceptionally isolated lone little doggie in the descriptive camp. Egoism won't tell you what you should do, and points out some problems in you telling yourself what you should do. That blisteringly frustrating perspective is good for a great deal of internal consistency, a strong link between ability and liberty. This is something lacking in most other schools of thought. As some point you will be asked if egoism makes everything okay, if it's okay to kill people because you want to. The question is malformed. I can imagine someone saying 'Since you think everything is okay, here's a punch in the face!' I can imagine someone doing it. People do all kinds of things. But if you need Me to give you permission to do anything you want, and if all you want to do is punch Me in the face, then perhaps you can understand why My estimation of you is sometimes unfavorable. Also within My imagination is losing friends and employment because I wrote a book on My own time that a few people read by their own choice that had ideas in it that some people disagree with. That's a thing that happens. The way egoism makes sense of the world is to say that the world doesn't make sense. Egoism is usually accurate in describing what people do, and says next to nothing in prescribing what people should do. Asking whether a thing is or isn't okay is asking what people should do or not do, and that's what egoism does not address. Asking if people do all kinds of things, egoism (and your everyday experience) will say yes, yes they do. All kinds of things that help you out, and hold you back. All kinds of things that are neither rewarded nor punished as they 'should' be. I can tell you exactly how to be an egoist. What you do with that information is outside My interests.

Egoism builds a shanty not a shelter on the plateau of heresy. Egoism stakes a claim and keeps moving. Most people muddle through the day. A minority seek to rule the muddle. A smaller minority still seek to reform the rulers, and a smaller number seek revolution, and a very small number repudiate the revolution, the reform and the rulers alike. Egoism is in that smallest minority, the imp of the perverse and the bur under the saddle, nobody's friend and it's own worst enemy. Egoism isn't the boy who laughs and points at the naked emperor, it's the boy who laughs and points at a naked empire.

You have to wonder (I don't) who is doing what in the act of self-sacrifice. There's a sour look on the face of so many altruists. They say to themselves "hey man, I gave up myself up to do what other people wanted me to do, and they didn't do the same for me!" Well, yeah. You got bullied by the golden rule. You got beat up in a game of "let's you and him fight." Start nosing around as to who stood to gain, who felt good about doing good, and you might find some satisfaction in selfishness. Egoism is a philosophy where it's better I fail at what I do that succeed at what you do.

My friends, I have My doubts about egoism. Sometimes My happiness is the happiness of others. I am bothered by lies, including My own. I think things and talk about things but don't act on them. I follow the herd. I hide My mutations. I am bound and fettered by space, time, money and mortality. I confess I am a failed egoist.

Yes, You Can Say "NO!"

to THE FUTURE

education God TELEVISION

Money Reagan AIR FORCE statistics

ADVERTISING COLLEGE *Marines*

MYSTIC EXPERIENCES TRUTH the past *Santa*

Jerry Falwell SCIENCE LOVE NAVY 'just-say-no'

TODAY Fundamentalism

WAR Work THE WORLD Technology

Philosophy yourself Family GOVERNMENT

"NO!"

The United States Constitution   A Friend in Need   BOX KNOXVILLE TN

YES YOU CAN SAY NO!

A Review of
The Myth of Natural Rights and Other Essays
by L. A. Rollins
Port Townsend: Loompanics 1983
Charleston: Nine-Banded Books 2008

The preceding illustration is not from *The Myth of Natural Rights*. It's a poster I made when I was twenty years old in 1986. My self-importance began much earlier but this poster was the first time I put it on paper. When I made the poster it didn't make sense, and it didn't have to. That's the funny thing about egoism. It doesn't always make sense, and it doesn't always (or ever) have to. When you sign on to Team Me, truth and consistency are guests to be entertained but are never *maître d'*.

It takes someone like Me to review the 2008 edition of *The Myth of Natural Rights*. A host of Great and Powerful Oz's petition an audience with Scarecrow Rollins, notably Ayn Rand, George Smith and Murray Rothbard. Each offers their defense or examples of natural rights, and each one is sent home wizened from the encounter. It's a real treat to watch the natural rights peddle by and Rollins spoke them one by one. Rollins' explanation of why there is no contradiction in acting one way and advocating others act differently is an especially pleasant read.

If there are no natural rights, then is everyone free to do everything? I'm able to do a great deal, and from what I can do I do only some of it. Rollins writes "My life is of supreme value to me." And regarding an argument for natural rights by Murray Rothbard: "If I can advance my life with violent interference to Murray Rothbard, why should I care about Murray Rothbard's needs? [...] Again, if I violently interfere with Murray Rothbard's freedom, this may violate the 'natural law' of Murray Rothbard needs, but it doesn't violate the 'natural law' of my needs." Turns out that while no natural right prevents me from visiting the greatest misfortune on my fellows, simple man-made law (or laziness) does the trick. Rollins wrote: "Real rights are those conferred and enforced by the laws of a State or the customs of a social group" and that's the gospel truth. If man-made law claims to be based on the 'inalienable' or divinity, so much the worse for man-made law. It's the guns and jails, taxes and soldiers that get the job done. Some guns and jails are preferable to others: "To deny that there are ethical differences between governments is not to deny that there are other kinds of differences between governments, differences which can be of great practical importance."

It entertains me to note contradictions in Rollins' work. On page 45 he writes: "There are no unconditional 'musts' or 'oughts,' no categorical imperatives [...] That is why, although I am an egoist of sorts, I nevertheless reject what Brian Medlin calls the principle of 'universal categorical egoism,' to whit, 'that we all ought to observe our own interests, because that is what we ought to do.' I say, to the contrary, that it is up to each individual, insofar as he has freedom of choice in the matter, to decide for himself whether or not to pursue his own interests."

This statement is worthy of Me. But on page 85 Rollins writes: "For an egoist, the only 'justification' for one's actions is that those actions benefit oneself. If, by means of reason, A concludes that he will benefit from living at the involuntary expense of B, then an egoist would agree that A is 'rationally justified' in doing so." Squeak squeak little wheel. I am justified in needing no justification, rational or otherwise. Acting on my most rational conclusions will include unforeseen consequences. Rationality is a fine motivator, but so are indifference, humor, revenge and simply doing something even to my own detriment for the purpose of keeping another from advancing his agenda.

Another funny thing about egoism is that it's funny. I'm experimenting with a new delineator between the left and the right: the left can tell a joke and the right can take a joke. It holds in the corollary too. The left gets bent about certain words and images that aren't funny and the right rolls with it. Meanwhile, the best comedians tend to be lefty while the best comedians on the right are... who? Egoism and humor go hand in hand. Perhaps philosophy was never about vindication or truth or beauty or justice or equality, and we should have been looking for laughs all along. Or perhaps when you get rid of the wheels in your head, you get a little funny in your head. Left and right share bed partners more often than polite conversation can allow. Do you call it eugenics or family planning depending on what it is or depending on whether your enemy supports it? Splitting sides based on humor is a good one. In My political nyuk nyuk spectrum, egoism is more of the left than the right.

Living without natural rights, without human

nature, is kind of like now but crabbier or funnier, depending. The lives of the egoist authors are generally mundane, while the lives of those who lived as egoists and didn't write about it are often full of fireworks (note to Self...). See the world as an egoist with this simple thought experiment. Lift your wet eyes from My words just for a moment and look at something. You're seeing something, yes? Were you to count that something, you would count one of that something. Where is the "one" in that thing? When you look at two of something, where is the "two?" You already knew that numbers aren't in things, even if you've never seen it put into words before. There is no number-essence. And even though you know numbers aren't in things, you continue to use numbers. The convention of numbers is like the convention of natural rights or human nature. They aren't really there but people keep talking about them as if they were. I'm fine with that (and Mine is the opinion that matters here) until the smoke and mirror crew sets up for another production of It's a Natural Right to Do As I Say.

Natural rights are in the same category of sleight of hand as Plato's theory of forms. Plato said that when we see a thing, we see only an imperfect echo of the thing. If we could but see it there is an ideal form of a thing behind the thing we see. That ideal form is the nature of the thing. Sounds good if you're arguing for the existence of human rights. We're all different and imperfect people, but there's a natural human right somewhere that is in the real us, and we all get a share of it. Everything has a cause, and those causes have causes, and those causes in turn go back and back and back until you get to a primal cause, a prime mover, an ideal form, a human right. Did you see the trick? Everything has a cause—except that which doesn't have a cause. The logic that takes you to an ideal form doesn't end with that ideal form, it takes you to a super-duper ideal form behind it, and so on. There's no particular reason not to say our human natures are similar but not identical and not shared, in the same way that our human bodies are similar but not identical and not shared. Human nature is a strange sort of nature that isn't natural to everyone. Since "natural" was supposed to mean just that—natural to everyone—it's no sort of nature at all.

Bridging the divide between what is and what ought to be has yielded some spectacular Tacoma Narrows over the centuries. Kant be done, friend. But build those is/ought bridges must needs be done, it seems. No other way to get those donkeys across the void, each one of those donkeys shouldering a satchel-full of wheels to set spinning in the heads of would-be eager egoists. Take this wheel, for instance: natural rights. Somehow, the is (nature) brings us to the ought (rights). Is there any way to divine what ought to be from what is? Or is it all "because I said so" in the end? Egoism has naught for ought. Things happen, and they are what I prefer or attempted, or they aren't. But these "things," and even more so what you prefer or attempted, they are not-Me, not-yet-Me or was-Me and thus a secondary concern if a concern at all. SUX 2 B U. Egoism is calling it like I see it. *My Way* writ large. Not even "my best interests" sits on the throne above Me. That would suggest a difference between Me and My interests, making "my interests" a wheel in My head. That would also suggest a knowledge of what My best interests are, which is fine to pretend but can you write down your exact complete individual nutritional needs at this second? How about now? Nature is the Nuremberg defense on the cosmic scale. I vas only followink orders! It vas my nature! Well, it's My nature to call BS when I see it.

From *The Myth of Natural Rights*:

> If there are no unconditional "musts" or "oughts," then there are no "duties" or "moral obligations." Which means there is no "morality," no "system of the principles and duties of right and wrong conduct." Morality (like natural law and natural rights, which are specific examples of "moral" ideas) is a myth invented to promote the interests/desires/purposes of the inventors. Morality is a device for controlling the gullible with words. "You 'must not' commit murder!" Why not? "Because murder is 'wrong!' Murder is 'immoral!'" Bunk! Murder may be impractical or excessively risky or just not worth the trouble. There are all sorts of reasons why I might refrain from committing murder even if I would like to do so. But murder is not "wrong." Murder is not "immoral." And the same goes for rape, robbery, assault, battery, burglary, buggery, bestiality, incest, treason, torturing children, suicide, canibalism, cannabisism, etc."

But you don't care about that cream puff stuff—let's have some real controversy! The *Other Essays* forming the center section of *The Myth of Natural Rights* concern holocaust revisionism. Where does Rollins stand in 1983 on page 94? "It so happens that I am a skeptic regarding the Holocaust in general and the six million Jews supposedly killed by the Nazis in particular." Rollins devotes twenty-eight pages to "The Holocaust as Sacred Cow." And where does Rollins stand in 2008 on page 160? "As of now, I am a skeptic regarding both the Holocaust and Holocaust revisionism." Rollins devotes forty-six pages to "Revising Holocaust Revisionism."

Third up in *The Myth of Natural Rights* is an updated abridgment of another former Loompanics title by Rollins, *Lucifer's Lexicon*. Revealing My own bias, let Me draw out some of My favorite zingers...

> Belief, n.: A fig leaf used to cover up one's ignorance.
> Born-again Christian, n.: One who has been brainwashed in the blood of the Lamb.
> Catholicism, n.: Christian Pharaseeism.
> Christ, Jesus, n.: The Meshugah.
> Crusade, n.: A jihad for Jesus.
> God-fearing, adj.: Afraid of nothing.
> Gospel, n.: The Tallest Tale Ever Told. The Cruci-fiction.
> Miracle, n.: A disaster that you are lucky enough to survive while fifty million other people die.
> Religion, n.: A cult with clout.
> Sacred Cow, n.: Food for freethought.
> Salvation, n.: God's merciful act of saving you from Himself.
> Soul, n.: An invisible, intangible, inaudible, tasteless and odorless—but marketable—entity.

... and one more...

> Cui Bono? Latin for, "Who can I blame?"

Hurry hurry, hurry, there's a barb for your backside in Lucifer's Lexicon. The concluding critical essays on Islam make sure nobody is left out of the fun.

The Myth of Natural Rights is good, you ought to buy it.

MY CROWDED FIST THEATER SHOUTING FIRE AT THE END OF YOUR NOSE

The egoist edict on freedom of speech.

BORN EVERY MINUTE

Roll up, roll up, freedom of speech is a big circus tent. All the freaks are alive, alive, alive on the inside. We've got speech and the press, association and behavior, drug use and faith healing, an orgy of opinion and a panoply of perspectives. See with your own eyes the Egoist as He bends facts and morals with His bare hands (step away from the cage, son). Property begins with ownership of self, and what is done with the self is freedom of speech. I'll tell you again that there are no natural rights, but standing in for that phantom are My free speech, social convention and good old Johnny Law. Ten minutes of your time to read, a lifetime to wash the taste out of your mouth, hurry, hurry, hurry, step right up! The free speech freak show escaped the midway more than a century ago when readymades and collage crashed the gate. Everything is art is what you can get away with. Roll up! Roll up!

CIVIL MASTERS NOT CIVIL SERVANTS

My preference is toward civility, and I'm the arbitrator of what is civil. Let's keep it simple, no need to get the law involved just yet. Civility in free speech won't go overly against the consent of the speaker or the audience. Publishing a private diary found at a bus stop goes against the consent of the speaker. Showing naked pictures of yourself to children goes against the consent of the audience. Most of the planet boycotts My writing and that suits me fine. Boycotts are so civil they make your head swivel and tyrants shrivel. Workers are free to express themselves by quitting if the freedom of speech of the boss in workplace rules don't suit them. Disinclination to self-incriminate or sign a loyalty oath, to tattle or to babble when a simple "I don't know" would do are all marks of civility. Drawings and stories aren't a bother to civilized me. How I wish I could draw something or tell a story and have it come true. I'd show you a thing or two, I would. In this world imaginary things that never happened do not have magic powers. On CivilityBook, Mr. Free Speech is BFF with Mr. Blasphemy while Mr. Obscenity gets the occasional like. Call me old fashioned (please!) but I'd rather you not swear around My grandma. She wouldn't like to hear you be mean about Jesus either but I won't get between you two about it.

THERE IS NO *I* IN -ISM

My mom taught me long ago that sticks and stones may break My bones but words will never hurt Me. She spoke the gospel truth. Having a discriminating taste sometimes means developing a taste for discrimination. I divested when diversity donned dull conformity. What was to be an opening of the prison became a changing of the guard. Yessir, there are some mean spirited jokes out there. I've heard them and I've even said a few. The civil response curiously includes both silently walking away and giving the speaker an oil-drum full of his own medicine. Free speech is worth every penny. I've heard and seen things that hurt My widdle feewings, but after a while I'm the ego making Myself still feel bad. Rub some dirt on it. Opinions are like cliches, everybody has one and they all stink. It's alright by Me if you're wrong about history or science. Is asking questions ever vervotten? Are you kidding? Turns out crime is already criminal. Hate crime laws exist only to make voters feel good about politicians who look good. Female genital mutilation, setting girls on fire for going to school, chopping women's head's off for being too Western—you might not want to call that Islam, but let's agree to call it sexism. It's right wrong a rude rib scores the same sexist status as mad Muslims on the diversity discriminometer. I'm doing what I can to change that, sugar tits. Everything is connected but not everything is equally connected. Let's get your priorities in order. Mine, to be specific.

IF IT TWEETS LIKE A DUCK

I have revealed My whim as the solvent of reason. No need to look outside My dictates for delineating freedom of speech from something even worse. I know it when I see it. Government whistle-blowing, treason, defamation, public sex, killing animals, bad art, outing, IP expropriation, paparazzi, parenting, fighting words, graffiti, squatting, protest, vandalism, one more bothersome young person with a clipboard asking me if I've registered to vote... I'll be the judge of which of these are freedom of speech. Ask and I'll tell you what it smells like.

SPACE INVADERS

You want to start something, tough guy? There's what I say about freedom of speech, then there's what the law says. Physical violence is usually the end of your performance art installation. The point where incivility becomes illegality is when a body goes against the consent of their audience and their property (self). If it's all for a good cause, I say have at it. And I'm the guy who knows what a good cause is. Don't you? But ixnay to the whining or exhibition of surprise when you get busted. Speak your mind and take your lumps. Other people's hypocrisy bugs Me.

INCONCLUSION

The world ends when I die but you might still be shambling around in the ruins. As appreciative as I am to those who suffered greatly for My freedom of speech, given time most of these squabbles do look silly. Men and women around the world are in prison for writing the wrong poem or doubting the wrong holocaust. I care about My freedom of speech and one expression of it, at times, is your freedom of speech. The freedom of speech fun fair is an ugly affair and this kuffar knows we have to keep it that way. If you don't like what I have to say about freedom of speech, you go be Me next time.

TRAJECTORY THROUGH ANARCHISM

1982 *(age 16)*: I find *Factsheet Five* and by way of that magazine I find Kerry Thornley. By way of Kerry and *Factsheet Five* I find many anarchist periodicals and pen pals. Anarchism seems smart, strong, right. Looking back, I used "anarchist" to describe what I liked and wanted and what was Mine. It's something about the sovereignty of the individual, or you can't tell Me what to do, or something unmutual like that. In the back of My mind I think that these ideas are so good that the only reason they aren't in practice now everywhere is that they haven't been tried. Or perhaps not tried just right. Or perhaps the ideas aren't widely distributed, and if people only knew about anarchism they would sign on.

1987: I find an anarchist poster on the campus of the University of Tennessee and by way of the poster I find The Alternative, an anarchist group in Knoxville. We talk and do things, but anarchism does not flow out from us like a river. And while we're all on the same team against a much larger and more powerful team, we certainly do bicker.

1987: I published "Letter from the Graveyard Shift" by Gerry Reith in My zine OVO. An early questioning of received anarchist wisdom.

> We must stop thinking in terms of issues, power struggles, programs, policies, and projects (state and social) before we are going to be able to get anywhere, and this means an end to most of what the modern anarchist movement consists of.

1988-1989: I attend anarchist events in many cities. I meet with anarchists in the South and on the East Coast. I am a guest lecturer on anarchism at the University of Tennessee. The same imp of the perverse that led Me to read about anarchism pricks up his ears when he hears a friend say how concerned he is that another friend is reading Ayn Rand. Not that the friend is signing on as a true believer, but that her books in themselves are wicked. Noted.

1991: I write "Anarchist: Think for Yourself," published in the book *Anarchy and the End of History*. A high point in nine years of letters, essays and art published in anarchist magazines around the world. *Factsheet Five* continues to create contacts for me, including an unsolicited letter from George Walford in England. I correspond with George until his death in 1994.

1992 *(age 26)*: I move to Portland, Oregon and find radical bookstore Laughing Horse Books. Make a friend who volunteers there.

1993: From a letter by George Walford:

You remark the scarcity of "real live human being stories" in anarchist literature. Very perceptive. But it's not an accident. Anarchism is not about people as we meet them, it's about abstruse principles and theories (and, even more, about the resistance these encounter). The real human stories appear in the literature at the other end of the range, in the popular romances, thrillers, love-songs and—perhaps most of all—in tabloid newspaper stories, which go to extreme lengths to personalise (humanise) political events. Your own view of anarchism has it that people should be free to do what they want. The overwhelming majority of those who have encountered anarchism have shown very clearly that they do not want to do what anarchists want them to do. They prefer to do what they are doing now. We have no reason to expect the others, when they meet anarchism, to respond differently. Can your anarchism accept this? Or do you feel bound to impose (however gently and rationally) your ideas of what it is good for them to do? The dilemma of orthodox anarchism cannot be escaped by 'practical living anarchy' within present society. We cannot live without taking part in society, paying taxes and supporting capitalism by our consumption, and orthodox anarchism condemns all of this. The attempt to live the anarchist life is a living demonstration of the arid, empty, abstract unreality of orthodox anarchism; it cannot be put into practice, it is virtually nothing but theory.

1994: My friend from Laughing Horse Books and I attend a meeting. The meeting is made up of people who want to start an anarchist bookstore in Portland. The bookstore is to be called 223. I offer to help write the mission statement, including a definition of anarchism. Not trying to define a thing into existence, not trying to exclude, not trying to control, just trying to clarify our goals and means and provide a base to start from. Having a definition of anarchism is discouraged, as it will be divisive and we all know what we mean anyway. Anarchism is smart, strong, right. I notice that in twelve years of being around anarchists, most of us are under thirty. Where are the older anarchists in a movement that started in the 19th Century? And what has anarchism done... ever? I work on a definition of anarchism for Myself, looking for the first time with any degree of seriousness into the history and accomplishments of anarchism for source material.

1994: From a letter by George Walford, responding to My essay in *Anarchy and the End of History*:

I have to say one or two things about the content. You ask one of the crucial questions: 'if anarchy is so great, how come we're not all anarchists?' You ask it, but you don't answer it, sliding off into discussing whether individuals can live as anarchists —also important, and certainly connected, but not the same question. Your omission is not surprising, for that question cannot be answered within the orthodox anarchism which your article accepts. The position is in fact even worse for anarchism than that sounds, because that is only half the problem, the other half being that some people, few but enough to form a movement, have become anarchists. A differential explanation is needed, and significant, enduring, social distinctions between groups of people orthodox anarchism cannot accept. Third (this one we've had before) [...] you blame the personal inadequacies of individual anarchists for the failure of anarchy. This does not stand up any better than blaming individual supporters of capitalism for the failures of that system. In each case the failure is sufficiently constant and widespread to indicate a structural source, something built into the position. The only way to get past that sort of difficulty is to move on to another position. Examples of anarchist successes will be springing to your mind, but if you examine them you will find that (so far as they are successes in any field other than theory and argument) they are not distinctively anarchist. This of course links up with the first problem raised above. They both arise because orthodox anarchism, far from being 'so great' is extremely limited. Not only can anarchy not be practiced under the state, it can't even be thought out as an independent social system, in any concrete way, without running into contradictions that, appearing in practice, would wreck the new world.

1994: I define anarchism as the belief it is possible and desirable to maintain the world's population at the current standard of living without government and without a period of transition from the present to an anarchist world. The moment I put the definition on paper, I ask myself if that is what I believe and I answer myself no I do not. Thus I am not an anarchist. I go to My anarchist friends to see if they can find an error in My thinking—they turn away from that conversation, and My doubts are not lessened for it.

1994: I read extensively in the works of George Walford and his peers. Walford rejects egoism, but the idea of the Mass Rationality Assumption hits home. People project their values on others, and this includes intellectuals. Intellectuals think that most people would prefer to solve problems with intellect, and most people are capable of solving problems with intellect. Neither are true. Intellect and reason aren't forbidden to most people, they just aren't valued as much as convention and passion. Assuming otherwise is what keeps intellectuals in the political minority.

1995: One of George Walford's best critics, David Mc-Donagh, writes me. David proceeds to poke holes in My thinking from that point onward. Looking into what David considers good thinking, I am introduced to the works of Sir Karl Popper. Popper's book *Conjectures and Refutations* causes the bottom to drop out of everything I knew about science, rationality, history and politics. David also directs me to "The Impossibility of Economic Calculation under Socialism" by David Steele, neatly skewering the possibility of a functioning socialist economic system even with majority support. I start reading about economics, amazed at how ignorant I had been before.

1996: Feeling free of anarchism and a little burned by what I now see was My own hooded thinking, I call up the imp of the perverse to see what other forbidden ideas might be out there. Ayn Rand is suggested, and I read her works. Having already shed one hood I'm less inclined to put another one on, and I do not become an Objectivist. But moving through Objectivism brings libertarian thinking to My attention. It's something about the sovereignty of the individual... but I've walked down that path already and don't sign on as a libertarian either.

2001 *(age 35)*: September 11th. The base nature of much of humanity stops being abstract and My appreciation for individuals who are basically decent increases. The idea that we can all just get along stops scratching on its coffin lid. The need for having hard men on the payroll to keep away other hard men makes sense. I support the State, the army, the police as better than the alternative. I start working in a homeless shelter.

2005: The imp of the perverse continues to slip books into My hand, emboldened by the importance I place on reading one's critics gained by My reading of Popper. Nothing seems more important than finding critics who will point out errors in My thinking—friends who think like I do never will. I read extensively about right wing politics and pay more attention to mainstream politics. All houses poxed long ago. That being said, when a fact or idea rings true I don't turn up My nose if the source is otherwise unpleasant.

2013: What am I now? I try to be a good man and keep out of harm's way. I hammer at the chains of religion and theocracy. My atheist efforts are small, but I've seen small changes from them and that is satisfying. I think humanity's best hope is the open society described by Sir Karl Popper. I lean towards the free market and small government and the sovereignty of the individual, but I don't see these as flawless or always appropriate. I barely have any agency in my life and certainly no social policy making power. Egoism entertains me, and so I entertain egoism by writing a book. Whatever I am, I'm definitely not an anarchist.

CO-REMOTING WITH THE THUNDEROUS

There is no context for the man whose name is tEN-TATIVELY, a cONVENIENCE. tENTATIVELY, a cONVENIENCE calls himself a mad scientist, a neoist, a SubGenius—Tim Ore, Karen Elliot, Monty Cantsin—a krononaut. One of the many publications by tENTATIVELY, a cONVENIENCE was titled DCC#040.002—dewey decimal classification number 0 (generalities) 4 (not used) 0 (no subject) 0 (miscellany)... just as a book with this dewey decimal classification number would stand entirely apart from all the other books, so does tENTATIVELY, a cONVENIENCE stand entirely apart from all other people.

Re/Search magazine requested a photograph of tENTATIVELY, a cONVENIENCE's tattoos for their "Modern Primitive" issue, but the photographs were not used. tENTATIVELY, a cONVENIENCE does not fit the profile for a modern primitive. tENTATIVELY, a cONVENIENCE has not modified tENTATIVELY, a cONVENIENCE's body to attach it more firmly to a tribal past—tENTATIVELY, a cONVENIENCE has propelled it forward to a sixth-finger future. tENTA-TIVELY, a cONVENIENCE's earlier tattoos consisted of a red and green brain over the greater part of tENTA-TIVELY, a cONVENIENCE's head (creating the 3-D effect of actually seeing into his skull), crossed arm bones over tENTATIVELY, a cONVENIENCE's chest and a DNA coil from navel to penis. Later, tENTATIVELY, a cONVENIENCE made a tattoo index of the various scars on tENTATIVELY, a cONVENIENCE's body. Using white ink, the scars received a representational icon to go next to it showing what caused the scar (a talking tree prop on the forehead, razor on the right arm, venetian blind on the left thigh, etc.). tENTATIVELY, a cONVENIENCE has appeared in public wearing a shirt that reveals his chest. It is not a normal chest, but one with six small Lupa-teats. Forbidden only by economic circumstance from actual advanced genetic engineering (actually not currently interested in pursuing genetic modification), tENTATIVELY, a cONVENIENCE has advanced tENTATIVELY, a cONVENIENCE's evolution in other ways.

tENTATIVELY, a cONVENIENCE does not look like anyone else. tENTATIVELY, a cONVE-NIENCE fashioned a suit of clothes made from zippers, which can be unzipped into a single, long strip. tENTA-TIVELY, a cONVENIENCE made a frightening suit of long-hair wigs of many colors and fashions, and had a shoulder bag made from a moon globe with a leather shoulder stras and a hinged opening (made for him by John Sheehan). With the understanding that 'mustach-es make a man,' tENTATIVELY, a cONVENIENCE shaved twelve mustaches onto tENTATIVELY, a cONVENIENCE's head to be twelve times a man (or twelve times more accessible to normals). At another point, tENTATIVELY, a cONVENIENCE shaved a ring of hair from the top of tENTATIVELY, a cON-VENIENCE's head, in front of one ear, under the chin, behind the other ear (by gluing hair behind the ear) and back up to the top of the head: the effect was someone with their face on sideways. tENTATIVELY, a cONVE-NIENCE has worn displaced false eyelashes and adhesive stickers instead of 'clothes,' peanut butter instead of makeup.

tENTATIVELY, a cONVENIENCE does not live like anyone else. His home defies convention. For extended periods of time the majority of what would normally be open space in tENTATIVELY, a cONVE-NIENCE's room was occupied by eight-foot diameter weather balloons; to navigate, one had to work around them. I had the rare opportunity to visit his laboratory in 1989. The front door opened to the back of a metal shelf, forcing one to walk sideways along a wall to enter the room. And to enter the room, one had to walk across his bed which was lying on the floor. Inside the room were shelves and drawers and cabinets full of experiments, documentation and equipment, all cobbled together from the least expensive of sources.

The biological processes of tENTATIVELY, a cONVENIENCE do not appear to be fully human. For five months as a teenager tENTATIVELY, a cON-VENIENCE did not bathe, brush the hair or clean the teeth, urinated outside whenever possible and often refrained from wiping the anus after elimination. tENTA-TIVELY, a cONVENIENCE has been a 'professional asshole' in medical schools, serving as a model in genital/rectal examinations, and taken untested drugs for pay during medical trials. tENTATIVELY, a cONVE-NIENCE has been known to ingest toxins and receive profound physical injuries without apparent long-term damage. No child co-created by tENTATIVELY, a cONVENIENCE is known to have survived.

Perhaps because tENTATIVELY, a cONVE-NIENCE is more, less or other than human, tENTA-TIVELY, a cONVENIENCE has demonstrated on several well-documented occasions the ability to interact with animals to a degree suggesting a special affiliation with them. One film shows tENTATIVELY, a cON-VENIENCE in a dog mask, walking on the hands and knees through the streets of London serving as a guide dog for a blind companion. When the two board a bus, tENTATIVELY, a cONVENIENCE is not charged a fee—tENTATIVELY, a cONVENIENCE has, in the context of the bus, become what tENTATIVELY, a cONVENIENCE appears to be. A videotape from the same European expedition has a nude tENTATIVELY, a cONVENIENCE wearing a Donald Duck mask to increase the animal appearance as tENTATIVELY, a cONVENIENCE communes with seals on the coast of Scotland. These otherwise timid animals appear entirely at ease near tENTATIVELY, a cONVENIENCE; they are intimidated by the camera operator more than the animal/scientist.

tENTATIVELY, a cONVENIENCE is a ma-gician, but of no previous school. tENTATIVELY, a cONVENIENCE has demonstrated, time and again, that with only an application of thought and effort the marvelous can erupt in the mundane. In December 1979 tENTATIVELY, a cONVENIENCE and several collaborators took two boxes of live crabs to a shopping mall in Baltimore, Maryland, where Santa Claus was meeting children. Prior to arrival they had tied the arms and legs of plastic babies to the crabs' backs. They released the crabs around Santa's cottage and stood back, watching the reaction of the crowd that gathered around the confused and weak crabs. "I'm glad someone's doing this," a woman was heard to say. The introduction of a random/ magical element into the mundane world of Santa's cottage at a shopping mall brought forth an even more random, even more magical response. The wizard gave a public demonstration of powers, and spontaneously a member of the crowd found herself 'understanding' it more, perhaps, than the wizard himself.

Mathematics has been advanced by tENTA-TIVELY, a cONVENIENCE. Using stencils, tentatively a convenience initiated 'folk math' on the walls of public buildings in Baltimore. tENTATIVELY, a cONVE-NIENCE engineered a perpetual pataphysical calendar, and has performed music on synthesizers by reading the parameters of a patch created by tENTATIVELY, a cONVENIENCE (the mathematical information holding more potential for the listener than its application). Grammar and diction have also been accelerated by tEN-TATIVELY, a cONVENIENCE: here is an example of his own script:

> i 1st met gayle at a halloween party in t he apt building turned commune
> in wch she resided in wash d c wch was temporarily housing
> a suggestion box i made t he ntrance 2 wch was made
> from a simulated cunt made from rubber.
> t he friend i'd given t he suggestion box 2
> was wearing a dildo on his head like a unicorn horn

& gayle (wearing a black leotard) was sucking on it.
later t ha t nite i wsa playing w/ a computer connected keyboard & CRT
when gale came in2 t he room w/ an approximately 8" in diameter
frozen wad of actual bulls' eyes
& placed them next 2 t he keyboard at wch i was seated.
i was impressed.
t he computer room had a couch in it
& i later learned t ha t some1 had spent t he nite in t he room
w/out having noticed t he eyeballs
& upon awakening in t he morning 2 find them no longer frozen
& scattered about on t he floor of t he small room
ran screaming in terror thruout t he commune..

tENTATIVELY, a cONVENIENCE injects humor into his reports by revealing the hidden laughter in words— the becomes 'tee hee,' that becomes 'tee ha (t).' tENTA-TIVELY, a cONVENIENCE has transmitted infor-mation via telephone, television, radio, audio and video cassette, vinyl and computer—no medium is outside the parameter of tENTATIVELY, a cONVENIENCE, but the use each medium is put to is always at the parameter of its abilities.

The most common mistake made by those attempting to classify tENTATIVELY, a cONVE-NIENCE is that he is an 'artist.' tENTATIVELY, a cON-VENIENCE understands art and has created art, but he is not an artist. tENTATIVELY, a cONVENIENCE has used paint, film, video, sound and words in his research, but the process of the research and its results are science. tENTATIVELY, a cONVENIENCE's attention to de-tail, tENTATIVELY, a cONVENIENCE's willingness to carry out the research far beyond any hope of personal gain or safety, and the quality of his documentation, give credence to the title tENTATIVELY, a cONVE-NIENCE gives tENTATIVELY, a cONVENIENCE: mad scientist.

Over the course of sixteen years, tENTATIVE-LY, a cONVENIENCE wrote down the word and phrases that appeared in the mind of tENTATIVELY, a cONVENIENCE while half-asleep. The resulting text was gathered into a book titled 'telepathy receptivity training,' and includes:

> blinkey modeling
> i can't see washing my hands in cake
> something backwards, you have to have one of those things and two of everything
> i call upon the rules and the grey moving sand...

For sixteen years work, the results are only ten pages of large-typeface text—not unlike the notebook of a bota-nist who searches for plants so exotic they are found only once in a lifetime. Few artists would be willing to present such a small return for so many years work, while any scientist would be proud of such dedication.

Another of tENTATIVELY, a cONVE-NIENCE's projects is 'mike film.' In the late 1970s tEN-TATIVELY, a cONVENIENCE conceived of a way to transmute a certain number of artifacts he had created into a context easier to transport and store and which lent itself readily to further research by others. tENTATIVE-LY, a cONVENIENCE made a Super-8 film of tENTA-TIVELY, a cONVENIENCE's art work, processed the film, gave away or destroyed tENTATIVELY, a cONVE-NIENCE's art work (in the interest of transforming into a mad scientist), and proceeded to cut the cells of the film into individual approximately 46,800 photographs. The 'mike film' (mike as an abbreviation for microscopic and suggestive of microfilm) was then bundled in small packets and distributed to individuals and organizations all over the world. The recipients were then encouraged to distribute the film in the most creative way they knew, document the distribution and return the results to tENTATIVELY, a cONVENIENCE. Every few years tENTATIVELY, a cONVENIENCE publishes a 'mike film distribution form' which serves as a scientific journal on the dissemination of mike film. Mike film has been deposited in art brut museums, launched from balloons, consumed, worn as pasties, hidden in national monuments, smuggled into prisons and dropped in the ocean. tENTATIVELY, a cONVENIENCE dreams (with advance knowledge of the future?) of an archaeologist discovering mike film and examining it under a microscope.

No fringe group will accept tENTATIVELY, a cONVENIENCE—neither will any reputable institution. tENTATIVELY, a cONVENIENCE has petitioned the international museum of the extreme, Ripley's Believe it or Not, to exhibit tENTATIVELY, a cONVENIENCE. So far, they have refused. A very small amount of advance funding or sales has supported tENTATIVELY, a cONVENIENCE's research, but for the most part tENTATIVELY, a cONVENIENCE has invented (that is, created from discarded items) the majority of tENTATIVELY, a cONVENIENCE's life support systems. (Actually, as of 2013, he works for museums for a living.)

What evidence is there that tENTATIVELY,

a cONVENIENCE comes from the future? tENTA-TIVELY, a cONVENIENCE has in the past affiliated himself with the Krononautic Society, an international and informal society of time travelers. tENTATIVELY, a cONVENIENCE seems exceptionally unable to assimilate into normal society while being entirely familiar with its customs—and yet year after year, tENTATIVE-LY, a cONVENIENCE survives and continues the research without funding, a steady income, and sometimes without a home. tENTATIVELY, a cONVENIENCE has exhibited the ability to change tENTATIVELY, a cONVENIENCE and tENTATIVELY, a cONVE-NIENCE's environment in ways that appear magical but are in fact based on a superior technology of tENTA-TIVELY, a cONVENIENCE own creation.

tENTATIVELY, a cONVENIENCE is outside normal definitions of benevolence and wickedness, although tENTATIVELY, a cONVENIENCE does have a highly articulated definition of both as applied to tEN-TATIVELY, a cONVENIENCE. It is difficult to evaluate the behavior of tENTATIVELY, a cONVENIENCE by any but tENTATIVELY, a cONVENIENCE's own standards.

tENTATIVELY, a cONVENIENCE lived in Baltimore for many years: after a completely successful experiment in creating a book and record store (called NORMALS & still in existence after 23+ yrs), tENTA-TIVELY, a cONVENIENCE has left Baltimore and is currently living in Pittsburgh. tENTATIVELY, a cON-VENIENCE has been spotted in several cities, each time sending out a progress report just before the circumstances of tENTATIVELY, a cONVENIENCE's residence are suddenly altered (sometimes by tENTATIVELY, a cONVENIENCE's design, other times by a host's intolerance of tENTATIVELY, a cONVENIENCE's experiments). While the rest of us advance backwards towards the future, tENTATIVELY, a cONVENIENCE is simply returning from whence he came. What will happen when the present and the future intersect, and the world of tENTATIVELY, a cONVENIENCE and our world become one?

tENTATIVELY, a cONVENIENCE:
http://idioideo.pleintekst.nl

MULTIPLE NAME IDENTITIES

Multiple name identities are co-incarnations, shared pseudonyms, individuals who exist in more than one body at the same time.

A few multiple name identities are found in academia. Nicholas Bourbaki has written several influential papers on mathematics since 1935. A number of men were Nicholas Bourbaki. The theologian Franz Bibfeldt was also a number of men.

Most multiple name identities are found in literature. No one knows who wrote the 1930 book *The Little Engine That Could*. The story is attributed to Watty Piper, which was the house name of publisher Platt & Munk. Many men and women wrote under the name Watty Piper. Kenneth Robeson was the creator and author of the Doc Savage character, who first appeared in 1933. Lester Dent and a number of men wrote the stories, all of which were published under the Street & Smith house name Kenneth Robeson. Three German men were Stefan Brockhoff, author of mystery novels between the 1930s and the 1950s. Kilgore Trout is a science fiction author who first appears in the 1965 book God Bless You Mr. Rosewater by science fiction author Kurt Vonnegut. Trout is modeled after the science fiction author Theodore Sturgeon, who in turn was born with the name Edward Hamilton Waldo. Philip J. Farmer wrote the 1974 science fiction novel *Venus on the Half-Shell* and attributed it to Trout. V. C. Andrews' 1979 book *Flowers in the Attic* was so successful that authors have published dozens of books under her name since her death in 1986. The author Wu Ming is several Italian men who have published books since 2000. Nicholas Palmer wrote the 1990 book *Fuck Yes!* under the pseudonym Rev. Wing Fu Fing. On a lark, author Tom Robbins signed a copy of *Fuck Yes!* when a Robbins fan handed it to him. This started the rumor that Robbins was the secret author of *Fuck Yes!*, a rumor which helped Palmer sell 50,000 copies of the self-published book over the next four years. *Fuck Yes!* tells the story of a man who says 'yes' to every circumstance that life presents him. In 1996 Palmer sued Robbins, who agreed to never again sign the book. Palmer said: "It's not just Robbins, the book is good. It has allowed him to take advantage of my anonymity." In 2008 Jim Carry starred in the film *Yes Man*, which tells the story of a man who says 'yes' to every circumstance that life presents him. *Yes Man* is based on the 2005 book of the same title by Danny Wallace.

Some multiple name identities are found in cinema. Since 1968, films which the director wishes to distance himself from are attributed to Alan Smithee. The Internet Movie Database lists more than seventy titles attributed to Alan Smithee. David Agnew is a name used by the BBC as a shared script writing credit since the 1970s. Bruce Lee died during the production of the 1978 film Game of Death. Two other actors took on the role of playing Bruce Lee playing the character Billy Lo.

Between 1988 and 1994, the Dutch composer Van den Budenmayer wrote the score for films by Zbigniew Preisner. Den Budenmayer was several men working under one name. Actor Heath Ledger died during the production of the 2009 film *The Imaginarium of Doctor Parnassus*. Three other actors took on the role of playing Heath Ledger playing the character Tony Shepard.

There is a species of human behavior that is not quite art, not quite politics, and not quite as presumptuous as all that sounds. I prefer the term pranks. I first learned of multiple name identities from pranksters. In 1960 the young Kerry Wendell Thornley worked as a desk clerk for the United States Marines. As a prank, he entered a false name in the training lecture roster: Omar Kayyam Ravenhurst. Over time Thornley and other Marines completed more paperwork for the non-existent Marine, giving him an IQ of 157 and fluency in 17 languages. Ravenhurst then got the blame when Thornley or one of his friends made a mistake on base. Thornley later wrote under the name Omar Kayyam Ravenhurst (and many other people) in the book *Principia Discordia*, and was in turn made into the character Omar Kayyam Ravenhurst in the *Illuminatus! Trilogy* by Robert Shea and Robert Anton Wilson.

A free music festival was held near Stonehenge in 1974. The audience decided to squat the location at the site after the performance. Eviction laws required naming each of the squatters, and so the squatters all adopted the same name to make the job of the police more difficult. Thus several dozen people became Wally. One of the Wallies, Wally Hope, was sent to a psychiatric institution for possession of LSD in May 1975. He was unable to detox from the forced drugging of the institution and died in September 1975. His free-spirited life and oppressive death was a central inspiration for a man to become Penny Rimbaud then form the band CRASS. Nabil Shaban later worked with CRASS. Unrelated is the Stonehenge built in Michigan by Wally Wallington.

Multiple name identities are found in the arts. Rrose Sélavy was an an artist and model in the 1920s, associated with a number of dadaists. David Zack has written about Monte Cantsin, who appeared in 1975:

> Maris [Kundzins] and I were in Portland [Oregon]. We'd been working with a Xerox 3107 that makes big copies and reductions. We were making giant folios; monster folios and dinosaur folios we called them. And one night Maris started fooling around with the tape recorder, singing songs in Latuvian about toilets and traffic. Well, we decided to make a pop star out of Maris. But it had to be an open pop star, that is, anyone who wanted could assume the personality of the pop star. This open pop star would be the most talented in history, better than Elvis Presley, Frank Sinatra, Sal Mineo and even Ry Cooder all rolled together in one. Pop stars have always been special to me, growing up the son of a symphony conductor the way I did. To me they stand for rebellion and acceptance, revolution and success and a whole lot of other things at the same time. We were mouthing Maris Kundzins' name, and it came out Monty Cantsins. Then we got to saying can't sin and can't sing and quite a few other things to give the impression that this pop star could be a thief as well as a saint.[1]
>
> One thing I definitely did invent is "Monty Cantsin," the open pop star. I did not do this alone, I did it in Portland, Oregon with the very first Monty Cantsin, an artist named Maris Kundzins. Maris and I sent a card to Kantor in Montreal, you are Monty Cantsin, the open pop star... I have to assert what Kantor did with this simple postcard belongs in any history of art and also any history of the world. The idea that people can share their art power is a very good one I think. My own un-

1   http://www.thing.de/projekte/7:9%23/cantsin_index.html

derstanding of Neoism is that it is about sharing, about bash: cooperation between people, putting egos and tempers aside. Though not always seeming to.[2]

Stewart Home has written about Karen Elliot, who appeared in 1985:

Karen Eliot is a name that refers to an individual human being who can be anyone. The name is fixed, the people using it aren't. SMILE is a name that refers to an international magazine with multiple origins. The name is fixed, the types of magazines using it aren't. The purpose of many different magazines and people using the same name is to create a situation for which no one in particular is responsible and to practically examine western philosophical notions of identity, individuality, originality, value and truth.

Anyone can become Karen Eliot simply by adopting the name, but they are only Karen Eliot for the period in which the name is used. Karen Eliot was materialised, rather than born, as an open context in the summer of '85. When one becomes Karen Eliot one's previous existence consists of the acts other people have undertaken using the name. When one becomes Karen Eliot one has no family, no parents, no birth. Karen Eliot was not born, s/he was materialised from social forces, constructed as a means of entering the shifting terrain that circumscribes the 'individual' and society.

The name Karen Eliot can be strategically adopted for a series of actions, interventions, exhibitions, texts, etc. When replying to letters generated by an action/text in which the context has been used then it makes sense to continue using the context, ie by replying as Karen Eliot. However in personal relationships, where one has a personal history other than the acts undertaken by a series of people using the name Karen Eliot, it does not make sense to use the context. If one uses the context in personal life there is a danger that the name Karen Eliot will become over-identified with individual beings.[3]

---

2   http://www.thing.de/projekte/7:9%23/cantsin_17.html
3   http://www.stewarthomesociety.org/sp/eliot.htm

I published work by Karen Elliot in OVO 3 (1987).

Stewart Home, in turn, has seen publications under his own name that he did not write. These include the books *Stone Circle*; *Harry Potter and the Quantum Time Bomb*; and essays including "Anarchism is Stupid: How Luther Blissett Hoaxed Bakunin's Idiot Children," "Communism or Masochism? An Appeal to All Revolutionaries Concerning the Rubber Slave Larry O'Hara," and "An Open Letter to My Avant-Garde Chums by Stewart Home." Someone anonymously suggested the (then) anonymous blogger Belle de Jour was Stewart Home. Not necessarily with his cooperation or consent, Stewart Home has become several people.

Spanning art and philosophy is the related concept of the third mind. Brian Gysin and William S. Burroughs encountered a third mind through cut-ups. Marina Abramovi and UWE formed a third mind through decades of performance art. Lady Jaye Breyer P-Orridge and Genesis Breye P-Orridge formed a third mind through surgery.

Luther Blissett (born 1958) is a professional footballer, manager and coach. His name was adopted by the Luther Blissett Project as an open reputation in the 1990s. Blissett the footballer is aware of the other Blissetts and does not disapprove.

Some professions are predicated on a lack of E-Prime. Observers and even the participants are unable to delineate who did what, how real it was, and who they are. These professions include porn stars, professional wrestlers and being one of The Monkees.

I enjoyed several people being Me in the early 2000s. A number of My friends in Portland were active at a website called irreality. They encouraged Me to join, but I had enough internet time in My day and didn't want to add more. Some time back I'd heard that David Bowie had hired actors to play his press agents, and that Bowie confirmed whatever exaggerated claim they made about him. Inspired by this story I encouraged 2-3 of My friends to set up an irreality account for Me and post to it as if they were Me, promising I'd confirm anything they posted as My own. For a year or two these friends would mix some of My own writing (from ovo127.com) with original writing of their own and post it at irreality. In the early to mid 2000's I met people who told me they liked My posts at irreality. I'd say thanks. Some of the friends I made on irreality are friends in the waking world to this day, perhaps only now learning I wasn't necessarily who they thought I was at the time. Irreality closed in 2008.

Every time we speak as if another has spoken, we lessen the lines between us.

The second-most influential multiple name identity is Anonymous. Anonymous began as an internet meme around 2006. Anonymous is also the name of many individuals who have appeared in public. Inspired by a character in Alan Moore's V for Vendetta, Anonymous wears the mask of Guy Fawkes. Anonymous has attacked major credit card companies and banks, communication companies, the Church of Scientology, the Epilepsy Foundation of America, Westborough Baptist Church and Los Zeta.

The most influential multiple name identity is St. Nicholas/Father Christmas/Kris Kringle/Santa Claus. Every December for over a century, Santa has appeared around the world, wearing the same clothes, carrying out the same actions, exhibiting the same demeanor, claiming the same home-base and promising to return at the same time next year. A significant part of the world economy is shifted when Santa Claus comes to town. In the late 1980s the Orange Alternative of Poland held a parade of seventy-seven Santas as part of their absurdist protests against communism. The SantaCon/Santarchy tactic appeared again in 1994, carried out by Suicide Club of San Francisco.

"You should never run out of people to be."
—Genesis P-Orridge.

LAN ASASLEM! THE UNIQUE ONE WILL NOT SERVE

> I have no need to take up each thing that wants to throw its cause on us and show that it is occupied only with itself, not with us, only with its good, not with ours.
>
> —The Prophet Stirner.

I. THE EGOIST CALIPHATE

And no need have I, just an impish impulse to impugn Islam. Not for the furtherance of faithlessness, but for the sheer sport of it let me stick My thick hands into the bees' nest. Yet fair dues, fair dues, there is a pathway from Islam to the Unique One for any Muslim who will present dorsal to Mecca. I am where I find Myself, and it tweeks My own nose to give the Religion of Peace a chance to redeem itself.

The ego, the Unique One, is not impressed by that which is other. Time being linear, that includes the unique one that I was. What I said remains what I said, but the I that said it has gone away forever from the I what is. The colloquialisms for this philosophy is 'making excuses for telling lies' or 'hypocrisy.' The term for this in Islam is Abrogation. The missives of Mohammed contain contradiction, which the Prophet resolved by making new statements which supplanted the prior (2:106, 16:101). Case in point: drinking wine is allowed (2:219) until it is disallowed (4:43). The Qur'an will tell you to not oppress others (42:42) and it will tell you to oppress others

(2:191-2). It will tell you not to compel others to be Muslims (2:256) and it will tell you to kill all non-Muslims (9:5). And all the while, "There is no changing the word of Allah" (10:64). The Ego both does and does not raise a glass to you, desert deity! None are fit to rule over the Self, neither democracy nor anarchy, and just so in Islam: "He maketh none to share in His government" (18:26).

Sentimentality and compassion are common supplicants for forgetting yourself. Islam spins away the wheels of distraction from the One. To the devil with children (63:9), wives (64:14), images (42:11) and music (31:6). Neither is the Qur'an hampered by rationality (2:118, 3:7), mortality (2:259), genetics (2:65-66, 5:110), archaeology (29:14), meteorology (38:36) or astronomy (54:1-2, 67:5). Did Mohammed invent a lie concerning Allah, or was there in him a madness? No, but those who disagree are in torment and error. 'Cuz he said so! There are mortal laws aplenty providing punishment for murder, and a body may find it prudent to observe them. But morality and the notion of capital-R Rights are philosophical phlogiston. When the Qur'an claims killing is kosher (2:191, 4:89, 5:33, 9:5) the scimitar of might as right is raised.

Islam extends a friendly hand to the libertine, what with the with wife swapping (4:20) and the drinking (16:67) and the freethought (18:29). Mohammed elevated himself above all other men and all other prophets, a stance receiving a knowing nod from the egoist. As an illiterate he wasn't trapped in the web of the written word, something that egoist Imman Dora Marsden would have applauded. Muhammed can hardly be blamed if his followers wrote down his sayings, arranged them not chronologically but from longest to shortest, and published it as the Qur'an (supplemented by the director's cut, the Hadith).

Bold strokes of individuality stand out in the calligrams of Islam. The Yazidi are to Islam what Mormonism is to Protestantism: older and newer, strange among strangers. The Yazidi peacock-angel Melek Taus would not bow to mankind, and for his egoism was cast out by Allah and is thus revered by the Yazidi. Iblis is bliss! The Khariji claimed that anyone could be a Muslim leader and the Najdiyya noted no leader was needed. Closer to home we have Yakoub Islam and the Noble Hakim Bey traveling a silk road from anarchism to Islam and back again.

Recite! I greet you from Jannah, the grand garden of perpetual bliss. Seated on comfy couches in the seventh heaven, seventy-two white raisins within My easy grasp, a bright white shining light illuminating the Unique One.

> "The Sultan has set his cause on nothing but himself; he is to himself all in all, he is to himself the only one, and tolerates nobody who would dare not to be one of 'his people.'"
>
> - The Prophet Stirner.

Ijtihad me going there, but... no.

II. ALLAH-TA BALONEY

> "Everything sacred is a tie, a fetter."
>
> - The Prophet Stirner

The I in "I" is not the I in Islam. Islam is submission, and the one wonders if slavery might be a better translation into English.

Pin back your hair and join me in pushing over the five pillars of Islam. I will not submit to Shahada, the declaration that there is only one God (Allah) and Mohammed is His Prophet. It's not that to do so would be a lie, but that it would be a tedious lie. I will not submit to Salat, daily prayers. There is no God, and if there were I'd trust Him to meet His own needs sans My supplication. I will not submit to Zakat, alms giving. Compulsory compassion is a poorly paradox. I will not submit to Sawm, ritual fasting. I have no sins to repent and am glad for my gluttony. Finally, I will not submit to the Hajj, the pilgrimage to Mecca. Seven circles of ring-around-the-meteorite isn't My idea of a good time.

Mohammed saw all the world beneath him as the perfect man and the final prophet. Yet he surrendered his throne to an invisible monster that lives in the sky. He ruled Arabia not for jollies but because it was Right—a right common spook with no seat at the egoist table. He crystallized the world into sharia law, eternally outside and suffocating the ego (particularly if you are a lady ego). Islam is for all the world, like it or not. Those who will submit are to be greeted as brothers, while those who will not submit are to be taxed or killed for their insubordination. Contrast this divine draft with the drafty designs of egoism. The only recruiting poster for egoism is My mirror.

The Qur'an is a cluttered collection of shoulds and shouldn'ts. From the Qur'an we learn women are to inherit less money than men in an estate (4:11); rub your hands in dirt to make them clean (4:43, 5:6); don't cut your beard or pluck your eyebrows (4:119-121); don't eat pigs (5:3); and speak only Arabic (20:113). In the Islamic tradition are required attire such as the turban and the burqa—the poor clothing of the pork loathing. The point on the minaret peak of our interests is that the Qur'an is telling us what to do. The Qur'an knows, it knows what is best, and it knows what is best for us— while not being us. While not even being Me, and that's a full time job with no openings. Egoism solves the is/ought problem by an unassailable IS and naught for ought. Islam? Call it Ought-lam.

Islam always and forever places the Unique One as a runner-up number two. All men are secondary to Allah (35:15), who does not love any man who loves himself (16:23, 31:18). For those trapped in the mosque of the green death, it must be awful to be full of awe for Allah. Egoism is indifferent to imaginary imps and their hurt feelings. In Islam the worst thing I can do is the first thing I can do—deny it (10:17).

III. CRUSADES WITHOUT CRUSADERS, JIHAD WITHOUT JIHADIS

> Only against a sacred thing are there criminals; you against me can never be a criminal, but only an opponent. [...] In all this the individual, the individual man, is regarded as refuse, and on the other hand the general man, 'Man,' is honored. Now, according to how this ghost is named—as Christian, Jew, Mussulman, good citizen, loyal subject, freeman, patriot, etc.—just so do those who would like to carry through a divergent concept of man, as well as those who want to put themselves through, fall before victorious 'Man.'
>
> - The Prophet Stirner

Mighty Mohammed himself suggests the appropriate course of action for egoists entombed in Islamic nations, and that is the tactic of taqiyya. If it is essential (or convenient) for a believer to lie about his belief, then Allah will allow it. I ask nothing more or less than this most merciful divine dispensation be divvied all 'round. Share this book with your closest friends, My friend, and I'll think none the less of you if you disavow it later on. In fact, let's pretend that My book is mulled by millions of mullahs in the Muslim world, most of whom will say they never saw the thing...

A djifferent djinn lifts up from the lamp in more liberal lands. The bait and switch compassion of hate speech laws can cause incarceration for correctly quoting the Qur'an. Tread lightly on your magic carpet, but make use of what freedoms you do have to laugh and point at the pedophile prophet. Here in the United States, where there are no hate speech laws, I am free to have no 're-spect' (submission) whatsoever for the religion of peace. Funny thing is, I have more respect for those rug-butting rascals than the distributors of diversity. The rainbow brigade bloviate that disrespect of Islam (and Muslims define what is disrespect to Muslims) leaves the meekly Mulsims no choice but chaos. They just had to kill people in international riots, you see, because someone some-where drew one cartoon, once! In contrast to the diversi-ty division, I think that when encountering an image of Mohammed, a burning Qur'an or a lack of accommoda-tion for each and every grievance the faith of perpetual offendedness offers that Muslims are able to decide how they will respond. They are not provoked, alakazam! into automatic murderous frenzies. That's a choice they are making. Just like the choice to practice female genital mutilation, throw acid into a little girl's face for the sin of learning to read, cousin marriage, honor killings, slav-ery, and oh, the list does go on. Like a battered woman who goes back for more, thinking this time she'll love her man into not beating her, Muslim apologists can't bend over backwards quickly enough to make sure nobody's feelings get hurt. That tolerance of the intolerable is the reason the weirdy-beardies are treated with kid gloves, allowed to have triumphant temper tantrums as they rama-down your throat their arid desert cult. If you want to shut down a bully, you demonstrate superior fire power. A book (or video or cartoon) isn't what makes these marching morons take to the streets, and I know it, and so I'm not going to refrain from—bombs? kidnappings? hijacking? TERRORISM? No, mean words. Ooh, so mean with the words!

I'd like nothing more than to see Mecca peaceably cleared out of the whirling whingers then used as a nuclear waste storage site, unapproachable by man or beast for ten billion years. Muslims burned the Library of Alexandria in 642, so if we burn a few Qur'ans then no loss is on the ledger. Legal bans on the burka chafe, but a silent scowl is sufficient. Muslims unable to work as others work and be educated as others are educated are free and more than free in the United States to found their own businesses and schools. Let's stop meeting them half-way, since half-way turns out to be all the way their way. I'm not worried about getting arrested for saying these things, although honesty might cost me a job. I don't have to worry about Johnny Law—only Jihad Johnny. Muslims the world over are commanded to not have non-Muslim friends (3:118). Challenge accepted! Let me help you with that. I want nothing more than what Muslims want. Mufti Abdel Akhar Hammad said the following about Egypt's first flowering of the anarchist black bloc in 2013: "God orders us to kill, crucify or cut off the hands and feet of those who spread mischief on earth. The President must give that order." Finally, here is one especially significant set of sutras that this kufar shirks. Muslims are compelled to kill me (2:191-2, 2:193b, 4:89, 4:91) while I am free to refrain from replying in kind.

> I shall be the enemy of every higher power, while religion teaches us to make it our friend and be humble toward it.
>
> - The Prophet Stirner

IT'S A SIN

There's unicorns, then there's the idea of unicorns. There's sin, then there's the idea of sin. The evidence for the later is not evidence for the former. This screed is the idea of the idea of sin, and rather than get mired down in the meta domain of your idea of My idea of the idea of sin, I'm just going to talk about sin.

Sin would be the germ theory of ethics, except germ theory explains something about the body. Sin can be measured whether the body is contaminated or not. When Dr. Other Person or Professor Social Structure says you're sin-sick, you are whether you feel it or not. How handy that they have a few bottles of snake oil left to clean the wound for you.

After the fact back-ups can be hacked for the origin of sin. (Tell us another story, grandpa!) Like this... thousands of years ago, people noticed that if you had sex with many different partners you got a certain kind of sick and those who had sex with fewer or no people didn't get sick in the same way. It was reasonable to think there was something about supernumerary sex that summoned sickness, and so sin was suggested. Sin stuck around after we discovered disease, but the if/then reasoning of long ago was sound. Or this one... homosexuals don't make babies and that's bad for the tribe, so homosexuality is sin. Or this one... if you have sex with a slave you might hesitate to dispatch them when needed and that's bad for the tribe, so don't have sex with slaves (especially slaves captured from other tribes).

You see the problems. A reasonable origin doesn't assure us a reasonable outcome. Sin might have begun as a pre-scientific germ theory. But let's keep that skeleton in the closet and not on display as today's model of how things work. Sin seduces us as a system, but the big picture turns out to be a clumsy cluttered collage. Nothing in particular makes some sex sinful while slavery stays satisfactory, or the inverse. Perverse, eh?

The secondary support for sin says while sin may stay a spook story, it stops certain situations society cannot support. Same sex marriage will sever the genetic heritage of some small amount of up to three percent of the population (heaven forbid the homos adopt or care for kids from past relationships), and to condone same sex marriage is to condone same sex sex, and some percent of the percent of the three percent of same sex couples who marry will later on divorce (a sin in itself), and for all this same sex marriage is living in super-sin. Since society says it seeks to stop sodomite and sapphist, call it a sin. Call it what you like, what society wants is secondary to what I want.

The third defense of sin is its divine origin. God made sure we had the motive and means to offend Him, as proof of His goodness (yeah, I know). I won't argue that because God does not and cannot exist we can ignore sin. I argue that even if God did exist, no authority outside of Myself is supreme. Roll, sinners, roll!

Fourth, sin seems selective in its sanctions. Eating this meat is sin but eating that meat is not. Sex with this one is sin but sex with that one is not. Owning slaves from this tribe is a sin but owning slaves from that tribe is not. I'm the arbitrator of the arbitrary, and inconsistency is not a concern. Lack of self-awareness about our whims is the worry.

Fifth, sin cannot tell the difference between the horse and the cart. Lusty thoughts co-occur with lusty deeds, but they do not cause them.

Sixth, sin suggests a certainty of nature not accorded to experience. Seduction is always a sin, slaughter is always a sin. Only the Self is eternal, and outside of Me all is in flux and to be evaluated by My entertainment.

Sin gets in the way of My doing evil, and doing good. Sin is compulsion of what I must do or must not do. I might set up a rhyming scheme to make My days more poetic, but even these epics must end. No compulsion of this world compels me. Secular sin should be shrugged off as silly, but sure enough it smothers smart people who should know better. On one side of the river the religionists are yelling 'heretic!' 'witch!' 'kufar!' while on the other bank the montebanks are yelling 'racist!' 'sexist!' 'hater!' You'll excuse Me as I dismissively drift downstream.

Humanists speak of natural rights, theologists speak of natural wrongs. Where sin is a successful shroud to spook the simpletons, wear it with a flourish. Otherwise resolve to absolve yourself.

OBJECTIVISN'T

The first Objectivist I met was in college. Now he's doing hard time for statutory rape. That doesn't advance My egoist argument against objectivism, but he was a dick to a beautiful friend so I'm going to spit while he's down.

I read *Atlas Shrugged* twice. The second time, I annotated My copy. I enjoyed it in the same way I enjoy listening to music at excessive volume. Do it too much and it causes damage, but every now and then it's a superb abrasive to scrub the brainpan clean. I've read all of Rand's books, three biographies and the main contents of the main websites, yet I am not an Objectivist. I comply with the order to turn in My objectivisa, never to visit the gulch again.

For all the books, essays, lectures and interviews Rand gave us on objectivism, she declined to write much at all about what it is. Plenty of examples of objectivism applied, but an example and a definition are different animals. Rand could give us an *Introduction to Objectivist Epistemology*, but just an introduction and not the epistemology itself. Galt's speech in *Atlas Shrugged* stands as the best candidate for what objectivism is. I'll paraphrase from the original ninety pages. Check your premises if you think I've misquoted the source.

Living things can either be alive or not-alive. For living things to act in ways that encourage life is both rational and moral, a union between what is rational and what is morally good. Plants encourage their own life automatically, and are unable to sacrifice themselves. Man does not have the automatic knowledge of how to encourage his own life, unlike all other living things which have instincts. Plants do not destroy their own roots, and birds do not break their own wings. Only man acts against his own self-interests, by sacrificing himself to others.

Were I listening to John Galt read that screed on the radio, that's about where I would have turned the dial. The world is replete with living things that sacrifice themselves. Many a virus will kill its host. Without programmed cell death, living beings made up of cells would not thrive. The first meal of many baby insects is mommy insect. Other insects go to bug heaven as part of the act of reproduction. Any number of animals will sacrifice themselves in a fight. Among those fighting animals are we humans. When Objectivists have a dog in the fight, it's reasonable. Objectivists say you shouldn't risk your life to save a stranger or a villain, but you should risk your life to save your beloved, because your beloved is one of your values (like rationality is a value), so saving your beloved at your own risk is like self-preservation. Presto-chango! But when it's the other guy fighting, that's anti-life and anti-reason. Life in competition is moderately well described by objectivism, but not parasitic life or symbiotic life. Everybody knows smoking is a pleasant and unhealthy hobby, but it's okay to be anti-life when it's so round, so firm, so fully packed. Objectivists want liberty and union, now and forever, one and inseparable. Altruism in living beings is unexplained to My satisfaction, and that includes the hand-waving of objectivism. Since non-false conclusions cannot flow from false claims, and since Galt's speech is Rand's one claim as to what objectivism is, full stop. Objectivism falls on its face, we can leave the rest there on the floor. Nah, let's kick it around.

Why violence is excluded from reason is more a matter of tradition than truth. Violence is unavoidable and therefore rational (to pretend there could be no violence is fantastic thinking). Violence even follows logical structures: if I hit that guy, then I get his stuff, except if he hits me harder. All men have an ancestor (maybe even a known ancestor) who killed to gain mate, meat and mirth. If those ancestors had done otherwise, none of us would be here today. Rand is against violent conquest except if it is Europeans taking the Americas, because the natives weren't using it anyway.

Objectivism sets rationality (and Rand) on the throne. While I say rationality means someone who can learn, Objectivists say rationality is a trait of someone who has learned. Having a good gander at a white swan, they'll have no truck with your black swan. Objectivism says once you learn tap dancing is good and short skirts are bad, there's no reason to check those premises. You're now a hammer in a world made of nails. Here's the list of compulsory reading, here's the list of forbidden reading. Here's the list of compulsory music, here's the list of forbidden music. How the list-makers are able to expose themselves to these ideo-toxins without harm to know they are inherently harmful to all exposed to them goes unexplained.

Objectivism claims it has closed the is/ought gap.

"Consciousness is ultimately based on perception." That works for Objectivists who can ignore the consciousness of those born blind and deaf. "The senses are valid." That works for Objectivists who can ignore sensory illusions, phantom limbs, hallucinations, mental illness. "Feelings are not a source of knowledge." That works for Objectivists who can ignore a the lack of a demarcation line between thought and emotion. "Truth claims come from evidence." That works for Objectivists who can ignore false positives. "The newborn human mind is a blank slate." That works for Objectivists who can ignore neonatal instincts like the tonic neck, the Palmar grasp, the Moro reflex, the Babinski reflex, blinking, stepping, rooting, swimming and tendencies to inherit the intelligence of one's parents. "The theory of evolution is only a hypothesis." That works for Objectivists who can ignore all the evidence on the subject ever gathered. For those Objectivists who can't ignore, there's always name calling, yelling, excommunication and other expressions of Randroid rationality. Objectivism says you shouldn't live your life for the benefit of another man. Okay. But that doesn't lead to refraining from asking (or forcing) another man live his life for your benefit. Objectivism is haunted by the spook of natural rights. Objectivism says a man cannot think when he's got a gun pointed at his head. But He can think just fine when He's the One pointing a gun.

More than anything, what marks objectivism as marketed to marks is its marked maligning of art. Heroic art is alright, and with that I agree. But then there's the morbid, the decadent, the obscene, and the functional. I've got no time at all for a Vatican list of forbidden books and even less for an Objectivist list of forbidden art. Insisting art must be for something is foreign to My mind. Agitating that art shouldn't exist unless it gets the Rand nod is odd. A bit queer, as was Rand noting homosexuals cannot reproduce through sex and therefore are hideous and repulsive anti-life libertines.

Like a religion, objectivism amassed adepts around an ascended one then shattered into schisms. Rand's champion Nathaniel Brandon built up a mighty tower to her majesty, all of which was struck down when (after stealing him away from his wife) Rand Objectivisted to Brandon getting some on the side. Schism the second happened when David Kelley willingly committed the unpardonable sin of telling a room full of libertarians that they were wrong. The problem, you see, is that Objectivists can't even talk to libertarians—that gives them sanction, condones their ideas and existence. Stoney silence is the only appropriate answer to apostates. Kelley went on to found the Institute for Objectivist Studies, which changed its name to The Objectivist Center, which changed its name to The Atlas Society, the joining of which precludes you from membership in Peikoff's Ayn Rand Institute for life. Membership has its penalties.

Objectivism is a nice place to be from. Read some Rand, it'll help you get your me on. It's a good magic show, if you keep your hand on your moral wallet. Go out and meet some Objectivists. They tend to be smart (or child rapists, or smart child rapists).

Nothing is more A to me than A.

INFINITE MATERIAL UNIVERSE

The universe is infinite. It has no beginning and no end, no boundary and no center. The perceived universe might have a beginning and an end, a boundary and a center. But what we perceive is only part of the infinite universe.

Infinity is enough time and enough space for infinite possibilities to occur. Worlds nearly like ours, worlds identical to ours, have existed in the past. Worlds like ours will exist in the future. Worlds like ours exist now, in other places.

What we perceive is not representative of what there is to be perceived. The laws of physics and causality are local phenomena. Travel far enough in time and space and they may change. Travel further and they may not apply.

The universe is the sum of all the partially-overlapping and contradictory regions of space and time. What is impossible in one time and place is common in another time and place. Infinite possibilities includes those possibilities where what is possible in one region and impossible in another will overlap. The marvelous will meet the mundane. Gradually. Suddenly. Just once. Today, tomorrow.

In some of the infinite number of worlds similar but not identical to this world, in places and times where the laws of physics and causality are similar to but not identical to our laws, there are miracles. The sick are healed, the dead rise from their graves, the clever are wealthy, attractive faces beam with flashing smiles and the tyrants (petty and grand) are enslaved as beasts of the field.

This might be that world. Gradually. Suddenly. Just once. Today, tomorrow.

REALLY

Let us suppose a familiar street in which at intervals there are trees. In broad daylight no one would think of asking, "Are those real trees," or if one did, the questioner's soundness of mind would stand a better chance of being seriously debated than the "reality" of the trees. On the other hand, it is probable that such question, if made, would prove genuinely nonplussing just because of its irrelevance, and the person questioned might make what would seem to be the lame answer, "Well, I don't know about 'real.' At all events, they are trees." They answer to all tests to which any member of the category "trees" could be submitted, and that is quite good enough for me. This answer is in fact, and in spite of its apologetic air, philosophically the sound one.

—Dora Marsden, The Egoist,
Volume 3 Number 12,
December 1916.

Society can't run fast enough across a million miles to shout in your face that you aren't yourself. Everyone and everything is responsible for your behavior except you.

If you're acting weird you must be high. If you're acting normal you must be suppressing a feeling. If you're sexually attracted to this kind of person you must have a hatred for that kind of person. If you live here you must not like people who live there. If you are an atheist you must have met a bad theist. If you believe in God you must be unable to accept your mortality. If you're rich (or poor) you must live in a capitalist country. If you're a criminal you must have been deprived. If you aren't ingratiated with an ideology it must be because you're ignorant of it. If you think differently you must be crazy. If you're acting like a man you must be a misogynist. Nothing happens just because it happens. Non-stop, night and day, generation after generation, something outside of you is pulling the strings, there's not a speck of room for you to be yourself and they're going to give you an ear full right now about who you really are.

Really. You say you want such-and-so, but is that what you really want? Is it what you really, really want? How about really, really, REALLY? It's water torture, it's the judgement of Solomon carried out on a deli slicer. The notion that you might be YOU, is unacceptable. So it's imagined that behind you is the real you. Behind that real you is the really real you. And behind that one? I think you understand how the game works now. If they can get their hands on those puppet strings they think move your head and hands and heart, they can make you dance to their tune. So it's off to the therapist, off to the re-education camp, off to the sensitivity training, off with your head. The only thing you're conceded is your ability to feel guilty.

The infinite regression of your "real" motivations is like a ticket to ride the rails forever on a train that stops only where other passengers want it to stop. "Real" is a value judgement like any other, different only because it is always judged as preferable. There's a ghost in your machine that makes you do things other people like or don't like, but that ghost has a ghost if it meets the needs of the ghostbusters. These minders of the mind/body boundary summon specters where a spectrum will do. I don't think I have complete and internally consistent self-awareness. And I sure don't think you do either, not about yourself and not about me.

As the helpful hands of normalcy try to pull me in half, mistaking me for a matryoska nesting doll with the "real" me inside, there is one phrase I hear more than any other. YOU MUST BE AFRAID. You must be afraid to be sensitive, you must be afraid to work, you must be afraid to die. It's mentioned as a motive but it sounds like a command. You MUST be afraid! They live their lives in the binary state of afraid and not-afraid. Fear is their standard, their measuring stick, and a sharp rap on your knuckles is sure to follow if you measure your life differently. They don't want to solve their problems, they want to perfect them.

My day goes easier not trying to figure out why people do what they do. The energy invested by busy-bodies in inventing a chain of cause and effect stretching from a casual comment to the big bang is energy I'll invest elsewhere. I don't want to play their game, but if I must I'll play it My way. When somebody thinks ill of me without foundation or inquiry, I'm under no obligation to disabuse them of their prejudice. Should it amuse me to confirm their bias then heck yeah, I'm that guy and proud of it.

"There is no phantom guiding me. Here I am, walking."
—Renzo Novatore.

Really.

SO YOU WANT TO MEET AN ALIEN?

The Skin Horse **and Other Works by Nabil Shaban**

Documentaries on the disabled can be difficult to watch. Not in the sense of such films being ugly. Documentaries on the disabled can be difficult to watch because one simply can't find them. Frederick Wiseman shot *Titicut Follies* in 1967. The film depicts the lives of inmates at the Bridgewater State Hospital for the Criminally Insane in Titicut, Massachusetts. Their lives were made up of being bullied, forced fed, sprayed with a high-pressure water hose and confined in unlit windowless rooms. In 1968 the film was removed from distribution and all copies were ordered destroyed by Massachusetts Superior Court Judge Harry Kalus. Judge Kalus said he acted in the interest of the privacy of the inmates. The following year the film was allowed to be shown but only to health care professionals. Wiseman appealed the decision to the Supreme Court, which declined to review the case. The film was removed from circulation not due to obscenity or national security but because it was accurate to it's subject. Superior Court Judge Andrew Meyer lifted the ban on *Titicut Follies* in 1991, on the condition "a brief explanation shall be included in the film that changes and improvements have taken place at Massachusetts

Correctional Institution Bridgewater since 1966." Today you can buy a copy of *Titicut Follies* from Zipporah Films, Inc.

No such luck for *The Skin Horse*. Channel 4 (formerly Central Television, UK) commissioned Nabil Shaban and Nigel Evans to make the 1982 film but Channel 4 does not sell it. No one sells it, not legally. Worldcat does not list it as existing in the interlibrary loan system. Exactly one private library in the world has it in their collection. If you are exceptionally fortunate you may have seen it one of the few times it has been broadcast on television. In the United States, that occurred once. The documentary isn't banned, it is merely unavailable. *The Skin Horse* is a documentary by and about disabled people and their sex lives. Not their secret longing and private thoughts, although these are part of the film. This is a documentary about sex, sex among the disabled, sex between the disabled and the able. All unattributed quotes are from Nabil Shaban.

Co-author and narrator Nabil Shaban does not skirt around the issue. *The Skin Horse* is an adult film, made by and for adults able to speak most clearly about themselves. Mere suggestiveness would not have succeeded in this film. Like the Last Poets or Valarie Solanas, the time for subtlety ended long ago for Shaban. When a person is just a little different from the norm, suggestiveness and being coy are more common. When we find a birthmark or personality quirk in a partner it stands out for a moment and then is gone. When one or one's partner isn't even considered fully human by some people, the time to beat around the bush ends. The lifespan of the average disabled person is shorter than that of the non-disabled. The average screen time of the disabled is measured in minutes-per-decade compared to the screen time of the non-disabled. A wink and a nod just isn't going to cut it. These are stories told once, and there's no follow-up special presentation later on. *The Skin Horse* is honest in a way most sex documentaries only aspire to be honest.

The honesty begins with a discussion of beauty. Classical Western philosophy said physical beauty is a virtue, like honesty or courage. Deviation from the perfect form was either a punishment or a moral weakness. The etymology of the word monster is that of a beast sent by the gods as a warning, a demonstration. In the 21st Century other theories of beauty predominate. *The Skin Horse* asks us to consider four theories of beauty.

First, is beauty like the sun, radiating from a center and growing cold with distance? Some sections of *The Skin Horse* support this classic idea. "Most disabled or deformed people I met at special school, sheltered workshop or crip college couldn't wait to go to bed with an able-bodied person. I know that to be true of me."

Second, is beauty is in the eye of the beholder? Perhaps disability does not matter. Those who are left handed tend towards mental illness, higher rates of suicide and imprisonment and shorter lives than right handers. But being left handed is not seen as a disability. Perhaps what we see as beauty or disability is arbitrary, a frame of reference we are free to modify or reject. This was the thinking behind the founding of the Outsiders in 1979. The Outsiders "is a vibrant social and peer support network of disabled people. We are many different things to our many members. [...] Whenever possible,

Outsiders works together with other groups to campaign for the acceptance of disabled people as sexual partners." *The Skin Horse* includes interviews with a founder of The Outsiders: "If I'd thought about it before I started I don't think I would have ever dared to do it because I never really thought it would work. Everyone said it wouldn't work. But actually, however disabled you are you are still able to love somebody and be loved. So the most amazing marriages and... pairings... have taken place. Despite the fact that they might not only be disabled but also homosexual. Goodness knows, they're just like anybody else." *The Skin Horse* also includes interviews with a member of Outsiders, Jack: "Everyone's got ability and disability."

Third, is beauty a spiritual force? Is beauty to the body as the mind is to the brain? Perhaps beauty and disability are not part of us at all, but a shadow cast by an inner light. Most of the speakers in *The Skin Horse* hold this theory of beauty. Shaban is a keen researcher into the paranormal, psychic powers, UFOs and utopian politics. Open the gates to a single taboo and the rest come marching in. "From childhood we learn that there is always more than meets the eye, that external appearances are misleading, that what exists within us all is always greater than the sum of the parts. [...] To admit love is to admit there is more to appearances. And to admit that we all have to work much harder at being human. We have to consider not only the body but also the soul." Another man speaks of sex as a spiritual experience rather than a physical one: "I know the joy, the contentment, the feeling of spirituality, the utter relief from the limitations of my body which comes from sex. Just calling it sex is a very limiting word. It's far more than people think with just one word. My body is very limiting but in sex I feel complete freedom." Tina Leslie talks about the difference between her body and her self. "Sometimes I eat in front of a mirror to see the mask as other people see me. And try to see their feelings. But this is what they see. It's got nothing to do with me, the real me, a lover sees that, the real me. But I still never quite, quite believe it. But my god, I'd rather this than some celibate martyrdom. [...] Some people see me as an ugly thing. They can't see me as a being, and as a sexual person, never. Christ, I don't mind being seen like that. What's the point of militant feminism? I like men. I don't want to take refuge in something disabled women use as an excuse suppress their sexuality."

And fourth, is beauty a fetish? Are some beautiful because they are different? Thousands of gigabytes of disability pornography are shuttled about the globe every day, lending some weight to this theory. Nearly thirty years earlier, *The Skin Horse* made the connection between acceptable fetishes (weight lifters and surgical beauty queens) and unacceptable fetishes (in a word, freaks). "Perfection becomes an imperfection, a curiosity, a handicap, and the handicap when taken to its physical extremes becomes an end in itself. Hence, King Size [magazine]. Jonny the Wad. Chesty Morgan. King Dong. Big Bum. And all those freaks we have learned to love and loathe. And some people lust after." Freaks have their place, but it is a well proscribed place. "In the world of sexuality, there are three genders: female, male and disabled. And what is more, traditionally, in the disabled group, we are categorized into monsters or children. Children, eh? So we're either monsters or children. We're either abused or patronized. We're either a fetish or sexless. Never in between. [...] It seem we need freaks not only to reassure ourselves of our own normality but more importantly to help us rediscover something. Perhaps that's why we create our own freaks in myths, legends, fairy stories, literature and films. Perhaps that's why we impart a certain humanity in them, and allow them to love and be loved. But of course only in fiction." Here *The Skin Horse* shows some of the approved and fictional couplings between able bodied persons and freaks, such as Leda and swan, a maid and a minotaur, Dr. Zira and Taylor.

If the disabled are (or would like to be) similar to anyone else in their sex lives, they may also be similar in their loneliness. One person in The Skin Horse says: "The problem of exploring one's own sexuality is a problem that everyone has." No matter how we see ourselves, the challenge in starting and maintaining a relationship (or getting laid) is in how others see us. One woman in *The Skin Horse* describes her days at the Home for Incurables over more than three decades: "Washed, dressed, put in my chair. [...] Sometimes I ache for the human contact that I've been denied. For a new face that isn't a nurse or another incurable. [...] It's this sense of waste that I resent most of all. It's as if people like me are somehow supposed to live our lives beyond frustration. As if part of accepting our lot should include the complete denial of any emotional life at all." Hey! you've got to hide your love away...

Getting off for the disabled can mean breaking laws as well as breaking taboo. One man talks about when his personal assistant brought him to a prostitute: "She was really sort of a bit freaked out by the fact that this guy carried me up the stairs and plunked me on the bed and said 'there he is.' I stayed there for about three or four hours. One hears so many terrible things said about prostitutes and I believe it's still illegal and all that but in that case in point the lady who I saw fulfilled a very useful purpose and I'm eternally grateful to her. [...] The events leading on from [hiring a prostitute] did make me much more relaxed and more self confident in myself as a sexy person, to meet other people, to make relationships, and I suppose over the last few years that has been growing and it's still growing."

Some of the men and women in *The Skin Horse* are still with us. Comedian Tony Gerrard continues to perform. The Outsiders still exists, and is the only place in the world that has *The Skin Horse* in its library. Shaban offers many of his works online at YouTube and elsewhere. *If I Decide to Commit Suicide*, *You Need Hands* and *The Fifth Gospel* include Tina Leslie, also seen in *The Skin Horse*. *If I Decide to Commit Suicide* is a video for Shaban's poem of the same name. It quotes from Eraserhead by David Lynch, just as *The Skin Horse* quotes from Lynch's *Elephant Man*. *You Need Hands* is a dark music video. *The Fifth Gospel* describes Christianity as 'body fascist' and shows Shaban and Leslie being patronized during a trip to the non-healing fountains of Lourdes. *Morticia* is available as a video-on-demand from amazon.com. *Morticia* is about a girl who wants to become a vampire. *The Strangest Viking* is online, a documentary narrated by Shaban on Ivar the Boneless, a viking who conquered much of England. An excerpt from *The Alien*

Who Lived in the Sheds is online. In *The Alien Who Lived in the Sheds*, Shaban shows that for all his fire and thunder he can make fun of himself. Shaban is a believer in the paranormal, but is aware of how such beliefs can look to non-believers. Shaban is an advocate of the outsider, but it not immune from gawking when he meets a fellow outsider. Shaban is his body, but his body is also a source of pain. Alien includes a film within a film called *So You Want to Meet an Alien?*, again one of his poems set to music and video. For all his success in the theater, Shaban has experienced one significant setback. He secured money for a production of his play *The First to Go* when England joined the war against Iraq. *The First to Go* is a play about the fate of the disabled under the T4 program in wartime Germany. Shaban returned the government's 'blood money' in protest against the Iraq war and the play has yet to find another backer.

The Skin Horse was where I first learned of Nabil Shaban, and I hope that this review can draw more attention to this singular work. But Shaban has done much more, prior to and since *The Skin Horse*. He has many stage, film and television credits to his name, some of which are listed below. He was part of the CRASS Collective and in 1980 co-founded the Graeae Theater. Shaban is an artist, an author, an animator, a director, an actor and a musician. He was the capitalist villain Sil in Dr. Who. He is a father.

Nabil Shaban has successfully scattered the ash circle that kept able and disabled actors apart. He is a man who can be judged on his talents. Shaban recently turned fifty and has many years of innovation and experimentation ahead of him. Thank you to Nabil Shaban for opening many doors, taking many risks and thumbing your nose at heresy.

Nabil Shaban: http://www.sirius-pictures.co.uk/
Outsiders Club: www.outsiders.org.uk

WHY SHOULD I SPEAK OF THEM?

The Strange Lives of Those who Sell Books to Those who Love Books

I had the great good fortune to be a used and rare book dealer in one of the best book cities of the world, Portland Oregon. The store I worked at that had the highest concentration of characters was surrounded on three sides by bars and was only two blocks from a rehabilitation clinic. Across the street was an atheist community center (where, in another incarnation of the building, the Kingsmen recorded "Louie Louie"). There were a steady stream of homeless people at the store, usually content to find a book and read in one of the back rooms for the day. But sometimes they had something to share. The Nazi was one of these.

   I saw The Nazi on the way to work early in October, standing in front of another bookstore. I thought he was just getting a jump on Halloween, because he was wearing a full Nazi uniform and standing at attention. He came into My store later that day, and the closer he came to the counter the more I saw his uniform was his own creation. He had taken a captain's hat, pulled up the top, taped a white rope around the brim, sawed off most of the bill with a serrated knife, and taped a drawing of an eagle & swastika to the front. His shoulder strap was the thin plastic cord of a child's purse or camera strap. He did have the colors of his shirt and pants correct, and a plastic eagle & swastika pin. His face and hands were mottled and large pieces of skin were hanging loose from them.

The Nazi pushed a shopping cart full of Harlequin Romance paperbacks into the store and asked if I could buy them. I think they had just come out of the Willamette River—they were not just damp, but leaving a trail of water behind the cart. I said unfortunately I could not buy them. He looked sad, so I asked what kinds of books he liked. "I like Nazi books" he said, and so I showed him the World War II shelves. There he stayed for quite some time (after moving his soggy books back outside). Eventually he came to the counter with a book on the German Air Force, the *Luftwaffe*. "Ah, here's one. Now I am only SS, but some day I will be Luftwaffe!" I told him that was great, and to work hard for what he wanted. He bought the book and left. I hear later he'd been kicked out of another store for shoving Judaica off the shelves. I saw The Nazi a few more times, usually in the proximity of rehabilitation centers. Haven't seen him in a while: perhaps he's met his goals.

A man came into the store once with an influencing machine sticking out of his breast pocket. It had a dial, lights, wires, and a brief set of instructions that included a verse from the Bible. I wanted to learn more about it, but he seemed self-conscious about the device so I let it remain a mystery. Another person had decorated his yellow and white striped shirt to read "I AM THE FREAK/WOMEN CUT OFF MEN'S PENISES TO MAKE THEM ALL EUNICS." I have never seen a more androgynous person. One man, breathlessly, gave Me the following note: "GALES CREEK. There is no record. It belongs to the state. It is no longer your because you lost your fair." Then he left.

Not all of the characters I've met in bookstores have been homeless. Book collectors and dealers have also stumped Me with their requests. One day a middle-aged man and his younger colleague came up to the counter and said "I only have one question for you: pigeons." What can one say to that? I told him where the bird books were and hoped that answered his one question. Another collector spent the majority of the day going through every section and nearly every title. He described himself as a stranger collector. He collected every book that had the word "stranger" in the title (except when used as an adjective, such as "stranger than fiction"). I asked if that was all he collected and he replied no, over the years he had branched out into "hospitality" books as well. And sure enough, when I was closing for the day he bought nearly fifty books with "stranger" and "hospitality" in the title. I like to imagine being the bookseller called in to sell his books some day.

Sometimes a collector or dealer would have an agenda for their buying beyond making money or acquiring books. On two occasions a couple came in and bought giant stacks of books on the Church of Later Day Saints, following a list of titles they brought in with them. The first couple stated they were saving the controversial titles from the Mormons, who bought them up to burn them. The second couple appeared the next week and bought the controversial titles without comment. Makes you wonder.

One of the primary benefits of working in a bookstore was being able to handle thousands of books without having to buy them or return them to a library. I had had the chance to read (and at times photocopy) kook books by the armload, books that may contain one diagram or chapter that is a real jaw-dropper but otherwise may not be worth keeping. I know enough esoteric book-happy types that if a book was really something special, I could make a call and get it into the right hands.

People leave all sorts of things in their books when they sell them. I've found a moldy bag of marijuana, money, book marks, photographs, postcards and, My favorite, letters and notes. Some examples...

> Dear Loren: This book is a loan—hope you enjoy it. Give me a call when you are through & we'll have dinner together. Love, Harriet

> Dear Dad, hope this helps you to pass the time while you are recovering. Love, Greg.

> Christopher, I you use this as a guide you will Read the whole Bible in the chapt & verse. Try to start & don't miss a day. I'm sending it & it still has my name on the Front. Love you. Grandma Rosemary. The Bible has a planned guide to Read the whole Bible.

> April 7th 1994/Happy 84th birthday Clara from your loving husband Harry.

> Why should I speak of them? It is necessary because of the extraordinary things they have blamed me for. And I? (deteste) (something like that) ridicule. Read, Read it aloud, and judge.

> Dear Karen: I do understand how difficult it is to say 'goodbye' and that extends to not only to friends but possessions, rou-

tines & just familiar landmarks. I'm sorry I got on your case about doing things. Your doing your best and accomplishing lots. I guess we both have too much on our plates at the moment. We're actually surviving alot better than I anticipated! Lots of things we've done/got will really help our transition into our new life. I'll support & help & understand you as best as I can. I love you Karen your a very special person and my life is so much greater now were together! Love Brett.

in the 1900 a million Penguin were slotered. they come up for air like whale they eat Krill. They swim like the butter fly. The penguins are marked with paint. Penguins swim up to 35 miles per hour. Penguin have great courge. they dive like olimpic swimer. The whole show is about

Inspired by what I have found in books, I have left a note or two of My own. On the back of a photograph of a young couple I wrote "I KILLED THESE TWO PUT THEM IN A HOLE IN CANYON PASSAGE" and stuck it back in in a book along with a postcard from Canyon Passage. I won't be around to see the reaction when that little treasure is found, but I can imagine…

TRIUMPH OF THE WILT

**How Weaklings, Whiners
and Worriers Wreck the World**

> If you have a suffering friend,
> be a resting place for his suffering—but a hard bed.
> > - Friederich Nietzsche, *Thus Spoke Zarathustra*.

> There is no virtue in suffering:
> to be relying on pity as a main argument is the tactic of the weak.
> > - Dora Marsden, *The Freewoman*.

INTRODUCTION

It's past time to stop giving passive aggressive a pass. Let us isolate and excise those who pretend to be weak and oppressed as a means of weakening and oppressing others. They don't want a leveling of the playing field, only an inversion of who gets to play king of the hill. History is replete with those who win their way to tyranny, but now we're suffering under those who whine their way to tyranny. A boastful Benito might brag about his bravado, but you better believe he will begin every broadside by being broken down and beaten, only now beginning to bounce back. It is a low-hanging fruit I pluck, but do read the appeal for autonomy, self-determination, rights and responsibilities, and most of all the woe-is-me pleas for ending the oppression, oppression, oppression found in the 1920 twenty-five point program of a certain German worker's party before they got the popular vote. There is no more sure path to power than to go from underdog to ubermench.

A simple test to tease out the agents of Grand Fenwick is to distinguish between shared grievances and victime du jour. The more novel the oppression the easier it is to set up a franchise for disenfranchisement to corner the concern market. For every advance in liberty a new dozen downtrodden must be discovered. Many misfortunes are lived by lefties, but there isn't a big sexy lobby for we sinister southpaws. Newspapers come in issues and old ones aren't news.

A shibboleth for the sympathy sect is the claim if someone suffered, they were in the right. Everybody loves a martyr when it's somebody else. A demographic over-represented in prisons compared to their percentage in the general population, therefore they must be the target of bias. That is the easier explanation than thinking they commit more crimes. Ladies are limited in leveling up the labor ladder, therefore the bad boys are bothering them. That is the more rational reason than suggesting women want men's pay without doing men's work. Sometimes people earn their oppression, or will eternally lack the means to escape it. All God's chilluns gotta suffer.

The victim's victory may be malingering as well as overt power, and I've got no beef with that. Today is a fine day not to work. If your aches and pains mean someone else can do the heavy lifting, then by all means do consider the lilies of the field. Maybe you don't want to use your usury to lord it over others, but wouldn't it be nice to lord it over your own time.

Somebody, somewhere, got put down and it might as well be you that benefits from it. When it comes to the rights of the individual it is wrong to judge them by the color of their skin, but when it comes to the responsibilities of the individual then the collective guilt of the oppressor is not to be minimized. All whites are racist, all men are rapists, so each individual black and woman is owed something. Plus ten times more for black women, and a hundred times more for disabled black women, and a thousand times more for lesbian disabled black women...

> "When pressed for a definition, I reply that justice is the redistribution of violence."
>
> —Butler Shaffer at lewrockwell.com

In Triumph of the Wilt I am going to identify several types of tin-pan tyrannies and the tricks of their trade. I hope I can end with some suggestions on what can be done to make the world less ugly, so stick it out if you can stomach it.

RELIGION

When a theist squeaks "you are oppressing me!" you can be pretty sure that means "you asked a question I don't want to answer." The very existence of difference in thought is taken as an active attack by the believers. They might confess to being wrong, but heaven help you if you are wrong in a different way than they are. I believe all kinds of crazy things, and things that differ from what I used to believe, so I'll let it slide that people think different from me. My brows only knit when the courtesy is not returned, and my thinking different for myself is re-cast as thinking for someone else. Buddy, it's all I can do to think for myself, I wouldn't think for you if you paid me.

The gaunt Galilean extols the undertow, and never you mind how the fairy tale ends. Jesus said "blessed are the meek, for they shall inherit the Earth." That would be the same Earth where Jesus also said He was the once and future king, who would rule with a sword, on an Earth where those that opposed Him would suffer eternally. Of course Jesus said none of this having never existed, but that's kind of the point. There's what the meek mongers say, and there's what they do. Christians flagellate their own backs only until they can put it to yours.

Hope is a different animal than faith. Hope looks at the roulette wheel, puts down its money and crosses its fingers. Faith assumes the wheel is rigged in its favor, and if it gives the hi-sign to the right pit-boss then in come the big numbers. It isn't called "hope healing" because that would tip the hand of the gambler. It's called faith healing, and children die from preventable illness and injuries in its name. To suggest parent might be a verb as well as a noun is to be accused of oppression. It's fine to neglect a child as long as you whisper a magic spell over the child as they die. Far better the little darlings go back to heaven than society tut-tut or tisk-tisk the caretakers for their superstition.

Claims of religious oppression tend to happen only by willful ignorance of real religious oppression. Muslims are killing Christians (and each other) every day all day in the desert lands. Let's hear a little less ululation for slight inconveniences or mean looks here in the West until such time as there is peace in the East.

SOCIALISM

Capitalism is known for competition over cooperation.

Businesses which beat other businesses survive, while those that undersell go underground. It's almost as if one guy has it in for another so that they can get it all. No so with communism. Communism emerges in the working class from the material conditions of history. That's why Robert Owen was a factory owner. That's why Karl Marx and Friedrich Engels and Vladimir Lenin and Mao Zedong were inheritors of family wealth. Because nothing says overthrow those other factory owners and dispossess those other wealthy families like communism. It's almost as if one guy has it in for another so that they can get it all.

There are nations what has and there are nations what hasn't. The disparity of wealth between the west and some African nations is great. Those less fortunate nations aren't shy about letting we the overfed know about their needs, and there's not a thing wrong with that. Where the problem arises is when Western nations or Western citizens donate goods and money to those in need, and those donations are redirected to the few wealthy men of those nations. Trillions of dollars have been poured into these nations, and they're certainly free to do what they please with that money. But when you're feeding a parasite and not a person it's time to pull the plates away.

Labor leaders lament that pay is paltry. We need a minimum wage, a living wage, and they wage war to wield it. So consider the scene. I've got a little corner shop and a budget for employees. I can hire one person at w-rate, or I can hire two people at half-w-rate. Suddenly all this talk of egalitarian employment sounds empty. It's not getting a better wage for everybody, it's getting a better wage for the guy I hire and nothing at all for the guy I don't. Let's see your union card, bub.

ECOLOGY

The race to the bottom doesn't stop with the lost boys. It isn't hard to find animal rights advocates that would put the interest of any pig over the interests of every insulin user. People for the Ethical Treatment of Animals have taken a page from Westborough Baptist Church by keeping themselves in the news no matter how foolish or insensitive (to humans) they appear. Keeping those big puppy dog eyes in the public eye is the fast track to financial triumph. When PETA passed the dog bowl around the congregation in 2009 they made $34 million. Also in 2009, PETA had a 97% kill rate for animals donated to its shelters. They're arfing all the way to the bank.

Then there's the deep ecologists who weep for the hurt feelings of trees and rocks. I have yet to find the physics lobby who will aggress in the interests of waves and particles, but that is likely my ignorance and not a lack of their being online. When the victim group you set yourself up as a representative of can't speak for themselves, whatever you say goes.

FEMINISM

A good deal of attention is paid to feeling safe in the workplace. Not in coal mines or among firefighters, not among those whose workplaces actually are unsafe by their very nature. Workplace safety is talked about among office workers and academics, among government interns and paper pushers. Those jobs that are unsafe by their nature may be improved by safety measures, but little is done to make them feel safe. The men and women who work in unsafe jobs understand that safety is not something one feels, but something one does. The closer to doing nothing one is, the more emphasis is placed on feeling safe.

Hippies and physicists agree: all things are connected. Where the dancing wu-li masters drift apart is the idea that all things are equally connected. Some feminists will advance that not reading 20th Century novels by men and women in equal amounts is related to why your friend got raped, but not as much as where your friend was and who your friend was with that night. Or is blaming the victim only okay when everyone is equally a victim? This is miserablism, a preference for pouting, because everyone can succeed at failing and that engenders equality. Morality turned inside out like a glove does fit the other hand, but once again that puts two gloves on one hand and none on the other—a curious kind of redistribution of resources that seems to follow the fainting flock.

Feminist fought for equal representation in education. Now women are the student majority in colleges in the USA. The budget for women's programs on campus only grows, never shrinks. Both in and before college, boys drop out far more than girls and boys are disciplined far more than girls. Feminists aren't fighting for equal representation any more now that they're the head of the class. Feminists fought for equal representation for women in the workplace. Now women are the majority in the workplace in the USA, and feminists aren't fighting for equal representation any more. Unemployment and underemployment burden men more than women.

Laws exist that protect the jobs of women who are pregnant for which there are no analogs for men. Feminists fought for equal representation for women in the military. Now women are able to serve at every level in the military, but women are exempt from compulsory registration with the Selective Service.

Feminists fought for equal rights for women in marriage. Now women initiate most divorces, most marriages end in divorce, most women who divorce are favored by the courts in alimony and custody, and feminists aren't fighting for equal representation any more. Feminists fought for the women's right to vote. In the United States men granted women the right to vote in 1920 but women voters did not share the right to vote with Native Americans until the 1965 Voting Rights Act. Women voters still do not share the right to vote with convicted felons, who are mostly men. Suffrage was a right for all until the sisters succeeded, then the number of humans included in that "all" shrunk significantly.

Feminists fight against rape. Men are the victims of rape more often than women, but because those rapes occur in prison feminists don't talk about it (except as a laugh HA HA!). Instead, the statistics of women who are raped are distorted so they come out as the biggest loser. Sex while intoxicated is rape, but feminism has abandoned its origins in temperance and does not fight to legally ban women from drinking (not even to legally ban women drinking while pregnant). Sex regretted later on is rape, no matter how willing a woman was at the time. Sexual harassment is rape, words and pictures are rape, questioning women is rape, lack of enthusiasm for feminists and feminism is rape, looking at a woman is rape, not looking at a woman is rape. Rape culture is however not at all the same as Islam, in which women have less rights than men, men may have women as sexual slaves, men may take multiple wives as property, men may have sex with their wives at any time (including as infants), no, Islam is not rape culture.

Feminists have an explanation of why women the victims, generation after generation. It must be the vote, except men voluntarily gave women the vote. So it must be the media, except magazines and television advertising dollars are majority funded by women. So it must be the internet, except social media is dominated by women. So it must be the schools, except from the classroom up and the administration down education is controlled by women. So it must be parenting, except at home and in the day care women are the ones raising children. So it must be PATRIARCHY. Yes, patriarchy, neither science nor sorcery but adopting the worst aspects of both. Under patriarchy men are rucking giant backpacks of privilege that they can never take off, only unpack an item or two on the demand of feminists. Under patriarchy women participate in their own oppression, an accomplishment as miraculous as lifting yourself off the ground by your feet. Under patriarchy you never need to demonstrate a causal connection between events, you only need to yell "patriarchy!" and you've made your case. Go on, yell it again for good measure. Patriarchy explains everything except itself. Why feminists can see it when others cannot, why feminists can move outside of it while others are trapped in it, why feminists exist at all when patriarchy is everywhere, these are questions best answered by a hearty

"Shut the fuck up! Privileged pig! Patriarchy!"

You must never think of a women as a baby machine, and you must never forget that a woman is a baby machine. Women need public funding to go to college but if they drop out to be mommies, that's okay too. Women are the same on the job as any man but if they need time off to be mommies, that's okay too. Put it all together: women need access to all academic fields to gain the specialized knowledge needed for specialized careers involving heavy investment from employers, but if they want to leave it all to be mommies that's okay too.

Her body, her choice! There's plenty of people and I won't sweat it if nature or nurture negates some nativities. We're a few billion deep in the miracle of birth and the performance is looking a little weary. What does wind me up is women who insist they have the right and responsibility to terminate a pregnancy while insisting the baby daddy has the right and the responsibility to support the sprog if they do not. And if daddy is willing to take care of the little angel even if mommy isn't? Or if the reveal of a paternity test might be testy, so let's just put on a brave face? Her body her choice! Vocal vaginal victim vindictiveness vindicates voracious vexation. Oprah Winfrey has had women on her show who were subjected to female genital mutilation as part of her advocating against female genital mutilation. It's entirely different that Oprah Winfrey also shilled for SkinMedica, a lotion that includes human foreskin in its list of ingredients. His body, her choice.

She stoops to conquer—don't you be a stoop and let her. It's a special kind of girl power equality. The strength that women admire in men has precedence over any other characteristic. That's why muscular boys, rich boys, powerful boys, famous boys and most of all bad boys catch a lady's eye. It's the most natural thing in the world for a woman to stay with and return to abusive relationships—which says something awful about NATURE, if you're unclear of my intentions. Either women are fit judges of who they should be with or they aren't. A woman held against her will should kill her captor, but a woman making what looks to the rest of us like a poor choice isn't asking for help. As the African saying goes, "if you see the dust of a fight rising, you will know that a kindness is being repaid." There's money to be made in intervention.

You won't hear this from rich red feminist lips, but there was a time when the Statement of Purpose for the National Organization for Women was about participation and partnership and (most heretical of all) both privilege and responsibilities. Feminists today don't even pretend to want equality with men if equality means equal responsibilities. It's all about oppression, and who is going to get to oppress who to redress grievous wrongs of yesterday or centuries ago or something. Empower every individual woman, but men bear collective guilt.

The penalties for false rape accusations are severe. Wanette Gibson accused Brian Banks of rape and Banks served five years before Gibson confessed she'd made it all up. Gibson has been forced to endure the shame of voluntarily sending a Facebook friend request/apology to Banks. Crystal Mangum accused three students at Duke University of raping her. They were arrested and expelled (but not before given D grades in classes they had previously been doing well in). The lacrosse team the students were on was disbanded, their coach was forced to resign, their remaining season of games was canceled. A cab driver who might have exonerated the accused was arrested because years earlier he had given a ride to someone accused of shoplifting. Duke professor Karla Holloway conceived an ad for the local paper supporting Mangum and Duke professor Wahneema Lubiano designed the ad. Seventy-two percent of the Women's Studies department signed on to the ad. But as it turned out, Mangum was not raped. Nor was she punished for the false accusation. She wasn't punished at all for her false accusations (but later when she killed a man she did get some jail time). The Group of 88 that signed the Holloway/Lubiano ad were asked to apologize, but, well... nah. Best to not back down from an instance of real institutional oppression when you've got such a great fictional story of institutional oppression.

In the UK, women who claim they are raped are compensated by the Criminal Injuries Compensation Authority whether the rape is found to occur or not. Men who are falsely accused of rape are not compensated. That wicked old patriarchy at it again, giving women incentives to act the victim and oppressing men for not being rapists as well as encouraging them to be rapists. When I become king, false accusations of rape net the claimant the jail time the alleged would have received.

RACE

In my world, chopping up the neighboring tribe with machetes is racism. My world is a tiny sub-set of the real world, in which telling the wrong joke is racism. In my world, cutting off a woman's clitoris with a non-sterile kitchen knife is sexism. My world is a tiny sub-set of the real world, in which an over-long glance is sexism. In my world, hanging a man by the neck until dead in the middle of town because he is homosexual is discrimination against homosexuals. My world is a tiny sub-set of the real world, in which failure to rush to the courthouse and the cathedral to throw rice at every same-sex wedding on record is discrimination against homosexuals. There seems to be a pattern of differences between my world and the real world. In my world, actively holding someone back (from remaining whole and alive) is oppression. In the real world, the world I see all around me all the time, oppression is not getting out of the way fast enough for the emperor as he struts the runway in his new clothes.

The Southern Poverty Law Center has the word "poverty" in its name, so you know they have to either be poor or help poor people. That explains why they have an endowment of over $223 million, I guess: every one of those poor people got helped and that's the left-over money. Floyd Corkins is a hater of hate and turned to the SPLC Hate Map for guidance. The Hate Map lists the Family Research Center as a hate group because they had lynched fifteen gay men in the midwest over the past two decades. Hey just kidding: the Family Research Center published unpopular and false information, and that makes them a hate group and so they go on the Hate Map so that haters of hate can locate hate on them. The restaurant chain Chick-Fil-A was also found to contain hate contaminants by the SPLC because they donated money to the Family Research Center. On 15 August 2012 Corkins bought some sandwiches at Chick-Fil-A and then went to the Family Research Center. Announcing "I don't like your politics!" Corkins pulled out a gun and started shooting. Later he said he hoped to "kill as many as possible and smear the Chick-Fil-A sandwiches in victims' faces, and kill the guard." If you're feeling the hate, the SPLC Hate Map is still online. Empowering victims to make victims, the SPLC way.

Kerri Dunn was a visiting professor at Claremont McKenna College in California. Her specialty was lecturing on race discrimination. Her car was vandalized with ethnic slurs, generating support for her cause. But the cause of the vandalization was herself, and the timing was remarkably close to the end of her contract with the college. Fortunately Dunn had 'initiated a conversation' and so her lies ended up telling the truth.

Thurgood Marshall encapsulated the triumph of the wilt in a conversation with William O. Douglas when both served as Associate Justices of the Supreme Court of the United States: "You guys have been practicing discrimination for years. Now it's our turn."

HEALTH

The dashing asesino Che Guevara is reported to have said "if you want a license to kill, hang a sign above your door that reads 'doctor.'" He would know. Physicians have sold us the cures for our aches and pains for centuries, offering nostrums for ailments we didn't even know we had. Female hysteria, bad humors, moral insanity, shunamitism, fermentation theory, zymotic disease, homosexuality as a curable disease, forced sterilization, these are but some of the known medical conditions that have passed their expiry date and aren't on sale any more. Take a guess at what medical conditions are on the shelves today—buy one get one free or else—that will be forgotten nonsense within your lifetime. I am not a physician, but I've seen some on TV. Take a quiet survey of what doctors are willing, eager and able to do to prolong the lives of others, and compare that with what meager measures they go to when it's their own time. We're being cured to death.

God grant me the inability to accept the things I cannot change, the power to change the things I can, and the bombast to ignore the difference. I say drink if you drink and don't drink if you don't drink. If you're a pest and a menace then you'll stay the same straight or snookered. The magic trick of deciding to drink then blaming the drink for bad behavior doesn't even get a slow clap from this audience. But the main irritant is recovery. That state of neither looking at the stars nor lying in the gutter. From what I hear, withdrawal symptoms from cigarettes and heroin is awful—and from what I hear, I can hear about it day and night. I liked you better high. Go ahead and bite some nails and quit your drug, just quit whining about it. AA founder Bill W. continued the this monkey say/other monkey do trend by decrying alcohol but endorsing LSD. Where AA waters down its drink with big crocodile tears is simultaneously serving as a court-mandated alternative to jail and offering no evidence at all that its program is effective. Keep coming back, it works—for them.

Prohibition is a temperance-tantrum. Like an arms merchant that sells his wares to all comers, governments that ban drugs can make bank enforcing drug bans. The same administration that urged us to just say no to drugs privately just said yes to Contra drug dealers in Costa Rica. Then as part of the war on drugs the generals locked away as many foot-soldiers as they could catch. The cold war on drugs is fought in the tobacco fields. The same government that subsidizes tobacco farms tightly taxes the tobacco trade while requiring warnings on the wrapper. It's so bad for you, have another.

Did you know some people simulate being sick for sympathy? That's sick! Being sick sucks, so they sign on the suckers. Brigid A. Corcoran shaved her head, strapped a sciency-looking device to her chest and told her friends and family she had cancer. Garage sales and benefit concerts were held in her honor, netting an easy $3,000 before her fib was revealed. Ashley Kirilow depiliated and was donated a trip to Disney World. And $20,000. Martha Nicholas also raked in the cash from a cancer of convenience. When she was caught, she had to give $100 of the donations back as a fine. Nice work if you can get it.

Some moms market their misery with Munchausen Syndrome by Proxy. Rather than exaggerate their own symptoms, they exaggerate (or exacerbate) the symptoms of children in their care. Susan Stillwaggon convinced her son he had cancer and got on the charity gravy train. Have no malingering doubts about malady, it's a way to manufacture money.

If you're blind you can have a highly-trained guide dog, or if you're not blind you can have a monkey or a horse or any other sort of animal, trained or not, as a comfort animal. Used to be a beggar would have to actually break his own legs to get ahead. Now you can get the paperwork saying you're disabled and you're good to go.

LOOKISM

I don't live my life as a criticism of yours. The amount of effort I have to invest in how you present yourself in public is minimal. Be fit and trim or fat and dim, it's your hot body and you can do what you want. Likewise am I not in the market to control your tattoos and piercings. Save your shaving secrets for another, and either go to the barber or be a barbarian—not interested. Would that I were aware of fewer that cared that I don't care, but so many get defensive to indifference. It isn't enough that I'm not going to not tell people what to do, I have to also like what they do. There's a limit to what I'm allowed to be attracted to and an even stronger limit on what I'm not allowed to be not attracted to. The rules are: be attracted to it but don't fetishize it but don't mention it but don't ignore it but most of all don't say 'no thanks.' Never judge someone based on their attractiveness, but always judge everyone attractive in their own way, because your way of judgment is always the wrong way. You can't win, and that means they can't lose.

GAY

I am not uninformed about the difficulties faced by homosexuals in the United States. What I am is unimpressed. It's crummy to get called a name, or not be able to get divorced. It's a measurable amount crummier to be imprisoned for life, thrown off buildings, set on fire, stoned to death or hung by a lamppost—the everyday experience of homosexuals in Muslim countries. The solidarity of the not-straight is strong, but stays Stateside. They are united by being Born That Way, but those brothers and sisters Born That Way Far Away... well, no money left for them after the vegan glutten-free catering served to the focus group of the minority caucus at the pride parade. Homophobiaphilia is a growing market. Once upon a time there was a gay movement, then a lesbian movement, then a gay and lesbian movement. Next came the bisexuals, then the transgendered, then the queer and questioning. Don't shut the door yet—there's also the straight but not narrow polyfidelitous, the kinksters, even the a-sexuals want in. It doesn't make sense that more and more people would want to join an oppressed group. But when you view the oppressed group as a special interest group advocating for itself just like any other special interest group it makes all the sense in the world. If you want to wield the whip, take it. But no more topping from the bottom.

Charlie Rogers was a supporter of Nebraska's "Fairness Ordinance," prohibiting discrimination against the non-straight. On Facebook she wrote: "So maybe I am too idealistic, but I believe way deep inside me that we can make things better for everyone. I will be a catalyst. I will do what it takes. I will. Watch me." That night three men wearing masks and gloves broke into her house and bound her to her bed with plastic ties. They used a knife to carve a cross in her chest and mean words on her arms and stomach. They tried to set her house on fire and fled, at which time she escaped to crawl to a neighbor's house. When it came out she had recently purchased the knife, gloves and plastic ties found at the crime scene, she said she did it to be a catalyst, to do what it takes to make sure gay people looked oppressed enough to pass the Fairness Ordinance.

Dayna Morales was a Marine, a cancer survivor, and a proud lesbian working at a restaurant in New Jersey. Some mean family left her a mean note at her workplace, disapproving of her lifestyle. And no tip! Donations rolled in, and Morales said she was going to give it to charity. Except the family did leave a tip, and no note. And Morales enlisted in the Marines, then went AWOL. And never had cancer. And the donations never went to charity. I guess we got our awareness raised or something.

LEFT AND RIGHT

Especially ensconced in powerless politics is the cabal of conspiracy theorists. Conspiracy theorists love being oppressed. They hold the big secret, but the subject of the big secret is so powerful that they are powerless to do anything about it. They have all the rights of bettering society and none of the responsibilities of doing so. This dynamic applies well across the board. Christians worry about satan, Marxists worry about capitalists, Muslims worry about Jews, small-time publishers worry about gigantic globe-spanning illumanetti. [sic] Or reptoids.

The left is lousy with affected affliction and no less rotten is the right. Socialists are sore about the mis-distribution of wealth in the world. They are welcome to give away all of their own possessions at any time, to crawl beneath the least of their brothers. Instead we see much green envy of the well to do, and promises that if we fund the revolution just a little more they'll be in the room with the workers when the vanguard closes the door. The right has fund-raising fear factories to make sure nobody else has any fun while blubbering about their own oppression. They don sackcloth and ashes and wail to the high heavens about indignities that they need not subject themselves to. Pornography, abortion, homosexuality, drugs, all concerns those campaigning citizens can easily avoid in themselves must now be forbidden to others. Hunh?

Gun control advocates can be found on the left and the right. When gun control advocates pass the laws they want in place, those gun control laws are enforced by police officers wielding guns. One more time again the pattern holds and repeats itself with repetition: to get in power, say you're out of power and take away someone else's power.

I've got a sensitivity to censorship. Free speech is worth every penny, but it spends better than the alternative. Whether censorship comes in the formal clothes of the feds or the casual attire of the culturati, you're getting chatted up by a group of people who say that some words and images and sounds are too strong to resist—for you. They are able to take it, but somehow you aren't. They can read those forbidden books to know that you can't be allowed to. Yet somehow the damage these denied tomes are said to cause never harms the censors. It's like the royal food tester getting a full spread while we kings and queens suffice with crumbs.

Ashley Todd was a McCain supporter in the 2008 US Presidential election. She said that while withdrawing money from an ATM a black man robbed her. When the robber saw a McCain bumper sticker on her car he said he was going to "teach her a lesson" and carved a "B" in her cheek. Presumably that's B for Barak Obama, but no explanation why he carved it backwards. B for backwards? B for Bizarro? Todd didn't have time to work out those details, as her injuries were revealed to be self-inflicted to scare up support for McCain.

An injury to one is an injury to all. That's acceptable by some. A benefit to one is a benefit to all? Well, only if you're the one. The union leader. The minority. The socialist. Life's been unfair so far, but if you just put your dollars in the collection plate I promise (way double harder than you got promised last time) that I'll come to power and then give it up. Democracy is magically getting the right guy in office, not practically getting the wrong guy out of office, so vote for me, vote for me!

PRIMITIVISM

It isn't always an iron fist in the velvet glove. But some dogs are so eager to follow the master's glove that they don't care what's inside. As long as the outside looks weak and innocent, the inside must be strong and wise. Call 'em a noble savage and you're a racist, but you can talk about indigenous healers all day long with no penalty. Heaven forbid you ask a local scientist or botanist or or cartographer or conservationist or anybody else how to navigate the jungle. No, ask only the aborigine about the arbor. Those without civilization are ipso facto presto chango the most civilized. And so tribes find it profitable to ossify. What might have been a two way street turns into a reservation with walls of white guilt instead of white law. Keep them natives on the reservation doing their ghost dance.

You don't have to travel far to find primitive tribes and their fans. The wallahs for the wise child fit this bill. A child's lack of experience and limited vocabulary guarantees their sincerity and innocence. It also guarantees that they can't complain or understand when adults exploit them. Every indigo child a Dalai Lama, chosen at birth to be a holy fool. Place your donations in the basket and, uh, we'll hold it until our little wise man grows up.

WHAT IS TO BE DONE

The universe got along just fine without you for a long time and it will do the same when you're gone. This is it, pal, hit the bricks and attend to your physical health. There is no strength in weakness. There is strength in strength. If you're slight of build and martial arts aren't for you, buy a gun and don't go to the no-go zones.

As you man up, the marching mewlers will usually self-select you out of the cool kids club. You'll also see some mighty crab claws reaching toward you as you pull yourself out of the bullshit bucket. They may want you to save them too, or they may want to drag you back down. It can be a treat to help a friend level up in this game, but while there's an 'owe' in YOU there's not a one to be found in I, ME or MINE. The act of compassion here is to cut them loose and set them free.

You've probably had a job where your boss is a jerk. He gets paid more than you, he has more authority than you, but you end up doing his job for him (and better than he could have done it). Sometimes that's just how it is, until you can manage to get yourself fired for you bad attitude. But for goodness' sake, don't seek out that situation. Don't do the boss' job for him, at a lower pay, with no authority, if you've got a choice not to do so. And choices you do have. You could walk out, or quit, or pretend to be ignorant and incompetent, or get together with your pals and start your own business. It's not unlike what works well with the big boss of society. Sure, there are historic wrongs and social structures that hold you back, and in many countries maybe for life. Not so much in the USA. I don't think it's possible to oppress yourself, but don't act like it is possible. You might not be able to stop society from treating you like a minority, but you don't have to treat yourself like one. There's nothing noble in being put down. The nobility is being strong in spite of being put down, not in being put down. Identity politics is like the dying part of martyrdom but with nobody around to change their mind about things afterward. Identity politics is an army of flags with no one to salute them but enemies—and that isn't going to happen.

Any adult can become destitute in the USA, but (except for the profoundly mentally ill) it's a decision to stay that way. Either one big drop out of society sort of decision, or a bunch of little decisions that alienated your friends and family such that they won't be there for you when you're down on your luck. There are poor on this planet who would be lucky to have some moist mud to munch on this evening. No food, no resources, no shelter, and nothing to be expected of them except suffering. Those poor do not exist in the United States. The wealth of the poorest in this nation would stagger a pharaoh of ancient Egypt. Potable water, roads, public libraries, K-12 education, and that's just a pinch of the free stuff. For only a few bucks you can get a personal telecommunication device with access to all the world's electronic information and any other person who has a phone. Don't use a hand-out to feather your nest—use it to fly away from where you are. There's no hard and fast rule for becoming and staying wealthy. But the path to poverty is well paved. If your environment is keeping you down, move out of it. Stop shitting the bed.

As for the fauxpressions, the concocted coercions, the dime-store despotisms—a cruel laugh is the best they deserve. The Triumph of the Wilt is in the whip-seat now, but watch as they tumble.

We don't have to fight for what our ancestors fought for, but we should be as strong as they were in case times get lean or in case someone wants to come take our stuff. Ask yourself what do you want to have happen, then make it happen. Turn your weaknesses into strengths.

Remind me I wrote all this the next time you spot me squat on the pity pot.

SHOT FROM THE EGOIST CANON

Egoism starts and ends with Me, of course, but you might think it has something to do with authors from the past. The orange thread I see winding through the following would be a heavy chain to many of their authors. This union of egos says something about me but not necessarily something about them. As for those I do not include, I offer them the bouquet or brick-bat they deserve. If you read only one book on egoism, it must be Mine. If you read two, read Mine and *The Ego and Its Own* by Max Stirner. And if you want to read more then come, the royal we offers an introduction to the me-nut gallery...

Our earliest example of egoism is Epicurus, an ally to be encountered in The Garden where the highest good is pleasure. Whether or not the gods exist or are good, they are of no concern: let us instead enjoy the simple pleasures of good food and a few friends.

Second Century Gnosticism is in the gneighborhood of the Ego. Direct gnowledge of God is possible, with gno intermediary gneeded. The God of this world, however is gno good.

Truth and beauty and laughs are where you find them. Once you read the Third Century book of Ecclesiastes (something a majority of Christians have never done) you'll wonder how in the world it ended up in the Bible. "All things have I seen in the days of my vanity: there is a just man that perisheth in his righteousness, and there is a wicked man that prolongeth his life in his wickedness. Be not righteous over much; neither make thyself over wise: why shouldest thou destroy thyself? Be not over much wicked, neither be thou foolish: why shouldest thou die before thy time?"

Royal greetings to that prince of books, *The Prince* by Niccolo Machiavelli. *The Prince* was circulated as a manuscript until 1537, five years after the death of its author. It was hated enough to earn an unfavorable mention in *The Merry Wives of Windsor* and *Pygmalion*. While *The Prince* is interested in the health of the State, Machiavelli was interested in Machiavelli and wrote what he did to earn favor for himself. Serving the State is off the table at the egoist banquet, but in the case of a Prince the self and the State are one:

> "Time brings with it all things, and may produce indifferently either good or evil. [...] How laudable it is for a prince to keep good faith and live with integrity, and not with astuteness, every one knows. Still the experience of our times shows those princes to have done great things who have had little regard for good faith, and have been able by astuteness to confuse men's brains, and who have ultimately overcome those who have made loyalty their foundation."

Consider the Marquis de Sade, who used his 1791 fiction *Justine* to write "Every strong and healthy individual, endowed with an energetically organized mind, who preferring himself to others, as he must, will know how to weigh their interests in the balance against his own, will laugh God and mankind to the devil, will brave death and mock the law, fully aware that it is to himself he must be faithful, that by himself all must be measured."

And then, the egoist wellspring: Max Stirner's 1845 book *The Ego and Its Own*. One Friedrich Engles said "this work is important" to his comrade Karl Marx, but upon a scolding by Mr. Marx young Freddy recanted his praise. K&F made a killing selling the bait-and-switch of material conditions both changing with the times at the individual level (no human nature) and leading inevitably to class conscious conflicts (human nature). The two also collaborated on *The German Ideology*, a 1846 attack on St. Max and his ideas. Ideas such as these:

> "Away, then, with every concern that is not altogether my own concern! You think at least the 'good cause' must be my concern? What's good, what's bad? Why, I myself am my concern, and am neither good nor bad. Neither has meaning for me. The divine is God's concern; the human, man's. My concern is neither the divine nor the human, not the true, good, just, free, etc., but solely what is mine, and it is not a general one, but is—unique, as I am unique. Nothing is more to me than myself!"

Friedrich Nietzsche did stare into the void, but only while holding the guardrails of good and evil. A superman that ought to be instead of is. But when he spoke of the Will, ah... "Man is something which is to be overcome. What have you done to overcome him?" (*Thus Spoke Zarathustra*, 1883) "He who must be a creator in good and evil, he must first be a destroyer and break values into pieces." (*Ecce Homo*, 1911) "That which does not destroy me, makes me stronger." (*Twilight of the Idols*, 1899) Trevor Blake's addendum: that which I do not destroy becomes stronger.

Max Stirner's wellspring is well navigated by Ragnar Redbeard's 1896 book *Might is Right*. Redbeard has a Shatner-like punctuation style also employed by Stirner-in-translation that can make reading the book—difficult. Other times...

> "Freemen should never regulate their conduct by the suggestion or dicta of others, for when they do so, they are no longer free. [...] The freeman is born free, lives free, and dies free. He is (even though living in an artificial civilization) above all laws, all constitutions, all theories of right and wrong. He supports and defends them of course, as long as they suit his own end, but if they don't, then he annihilates them by the easiest and most direct method."

I estimate *Might is Right* as among the most elite of egoist essentials. Do give it a go, in the edition edited by Darrell W. Condor if you can. See also *I Beheld Desmond as Lightning Fall—to Chicago!* by Conder (2007), a superb biography of Mr. Redbeard.

John Erwin McCall published excerpts from Redbeard's book in London. McCall also served as editor of *The Eagle and the Serpent* (1898—1902).

> "In a world whose characteristics were prevailingly 'lovely,' love would best become a man, but in a world whose leading features are to the last degree unlovely, hypocritical and hateful, hate is the only sentiment an honest man can entertain. Hence it follows that in this predominantly hateful world, men of hate leave their impress on every page of history, while men of love, with their pale and ineffectual negations, have their day and cease to be."

Underworld Amusements has in an act of unparallelled

generosity reprinted many rare essays from The Eagle and the Serpent under the title *A Bible Not Borrowed from the Neighbors*.

The Book of the Law by Aleister Crowley "lays down a simple Code of Conduct. Do what thou wilt shall be the whole of the Law." Crowley credited a deity named Aiwass as the author of this 1904 book, but as far as my field agents have determined it was Crowley who cashed the checks. Read on, seeker. "Thou hast no right but to do thy will. Do that, and no other shall say nay. For pure will, unassuaged of purpose, delivered from the lust of result, is every way perfect." How close to egoism Crowley was with the Law, with the notion all events are equally lawful. But then the black skies are filled with wheels of stars. Flickering fairy lamps of nature, the law of our growth, lawful acts and right events. The Beast did not step boldly into the chaos. As Aiwass saying, close but no cigar.

Jack London was a socialist. He portrayed Wolf Larson as a villain in *The Sea Wolf* (1904), But of course the bad guys have all the best lines. "Feet with which to clutch the ground, legs to stand on and help withstand, while with arms and hands, teeth and nails, I struggle to kill and not be killed."

George Palante was a sociologist but no socialist (although when it served him he stood as a socialist candidate). His individualism was of the aristocratic rather than democratic bloodline. In issue 323 of *L'Anarchie* (15 June 1911) he wrote:

> "As is the case elsewhere, the tendency to underestimate the individual has made itself felt in the intellectual field. Solitary thought—invention—has been depreciated to the profit of

collective thought—imitation—preached under the eternal word of solidarity... The result of this tendency is that we no longer exist and think for ourselves. We think according to hearsay and slogans."

Two years earlier in *La Sensibilité Individualiste* he wrote:

"The words anarchism and individualism are frequently used as synonyms... Individualism is the sentiment of a profound, irreducible antinomy between the individual and society. The individualist is he who, by virtue of his temperament, is predisposed to feel in a particularly acute fashion the ineluctable disharmonies between his intimate being and his social milieu. At the same time, he is a man for whom life has reserved some decisive occasion to remark this disharmony. Whether through brutality, or the continuity of his experiences, for him it has become clear that for the individual society is a perpetual creator of constraints, humiliations and miseries, a kind of continuous generation of human pain... Anarchism is an exaggerated and mad idealism. Individualism is summed up in a trait common to Schopenhauer and Stirner: a pitiless realism. It arrives at what a German writer calls a complete 'dis-idealization' (*Entidealisierung*) of life and society."

Dora Marsden signed in as a suffragette when the Women's Social and Political Union promised individual liberty for women. She signed out when the individual women were lost in a forest of feminism. In her magazines *The Freewoman*, *The New Freewoman* and *The Egoist* (1911—1919) Marsden made mincemeat of constricting causes, limiting language and self-censorship.

"The centre of the Universe lies in the desire of the individual, and the Universe for the individual has no meaning apart from their individual satisfactions, a means to an end... The few individual women before mentioned maintain that their only fitting description is that of Individual: Ends-in-themselves. They are Egoists... The intensive satisfaction of Self is for the individual the one goal in life... There is only one person concerned in the freeing of individuals: and that is the person who wears and feels and resents the shackles. Shackles must be burst off: if they are cut away from outside, they will immediately reform, as those whose cause is 'our poor sisters' and 'poor brothers' will find... A very limited number of individual women are emphasizing the fact that the first thing to be taken into account with regard to them is that they are individuals and can not be lumped together into a class, a sex, or a 'movement.' They—this small number—regard themselves neither as wives, mothers, spinsters, women, nor men. They are themselves, each cut off from and differing from the rest. What each is and what each requires she proposes to find by looking into her own wants—not 'class' or 'race' wants."

Tarzan of the Apes (1912) and *Jungle Tales of Tarzan* (1919) are popular reads with an egoist subtext. Edgar Rice Burrough's character Tarzan is the only man in a tribe of apes, able to be as savage as they are to survive (and amuse himself) while never unaware that he is unique among them.

> "In all the jungle, or above it, or upon the running waters, or the sleeping waters, or upon the big water, or the little water, there is none so great as Tarzan. Tarzan is greater than the Mangani; he is greater than the Gomangani. With his own hands he has slain Numa, the lion, and Sheeta, the panther; there is none so great as Tarzan. Tarzan is greater than God. See!"

DADA! DADA! DADA! DADADADADA-DADADADADADADA! 1916.

H. L. Mencken, Mark Twain, Al Capp and Frank Zappa were as unkind to radicals as they were to reactionaries. Each a journalist of their times, they have experienced differing levels of social opprobrium accordingly. I personally have never met a Mencken quote I didn't like:

> "The most dangerous man to any government is the man who is able to think things out for himself, without regard to the prevailing superstitions and taboos. Almost inevitably he comes to the conclusion that the government he lives under is dishonest, insane and intolerable, and so, if he is romantic, he tries to change it. And even if he is not romantic personally he is very apt to spread discontent among those who are." (*The Smart Set*, 1919)

> "Every normal man must be tempted, at times, to spit upon his hands, hoist the black flag, and begin slitting throats." (*Prejudices, First Series*, 1919.)

Fascism wasn't the only form of anti-communism to come out of Italy. There was also illegalism, the committing of criminal acts as a lifestyle choice. Among these bandit chiefs was Renzo Novatore, whose thrust toward the creative nothing pierces us yet. "Anarchist individualism as we understand it—and I say we because a substantial handful of friends think this like me—is hostile to every school and every party, every churchly and dogmatic moral, as well as every more or less academic imbecility. Every form of discipline, rule and pedantry is repulsive to the sincere nobility of our vagabond and rebellious restlessness!" (*Anarchist Individualism in the Social Revolution*, 1919). The Yomango of Barcelona carry on the illegalist tradition.

Surrealism slept with socialism and got slandered as a goofy do-gooder. But in its earliest phase Andre Breton and company made interesting inroads to individualism. Surrealism is not a dream-world, it is a rejection of differentiating between the dream world and the waking world. In this neither rational nor irrational but a-rational mode of thought, egoism operates the surgery uniting an umbrella and a sewing machine. Mad Love is the love for Me. From the *Declaration of 27 January 1925*:

> "Surrealism is not a new or an easier means of expression nor even a metaphysics of poetry. It is a means of total liberation of the mind and all that resembles it. We do not pretend to change the mores of men, but we intend to show the fragility of their thought and on what shifting foundations, what caverns, they have built their trembling houses. At each turn of its thought, society will find us waiting."

Individual Liberty by Benjamin Tucker was published in 1926, made up of individualist anarchist essays written four decades earlier. Anarchism as an alleviation to all ailments was already an anachronism. "Forty years ago, when the foregoing essay was written... the Anarchistic remedy was still applicable... Our civilization is in its death throes. We may last a couple of centuries yet; on the other hand, a decade may precipitate our finish." Tucker got tuckered out fighting for other people's freedom and you'd think at some point he would have learned his lesson. When he spoke for himself I'd give him a listen. From *Instead of a Book*:

> "So far as inherent right is concerned, might is its only measure. Any man, be his name Bill Sykes or Alexander Romanoff, and any set of men, whether the Chinese highbinders or the Congress of the United States, have the right, if they have the power, to kill or coerce other men and to make the entire world subservient to their ends. Society's right to enslave the individual

and the individual's right to enslave society are unequal only because their powers are unequal."

There is only one Malfew Seklew and Sirfessor F. Wilkesbarre is his prophet. The Laughing Philosopher of Lancastershire was the transmitter of the ego nature to the United States by way of his 1927 book *The Gospel of Malfew Seklew.*

"Egoism is the law of the Ego. It is a secret of man, not a secret of Nature; because Nature exposes her purpose in the actions of every human being, and every other living thing. [...] Certain men, who have had the courage to probe down to the very bottom of their own minds, have come to the conclusion that self-interest is the one motive of all human action; I might say of all action that is not merely mechanical and has life at the root of it. This belief, conviction, or conclusion—term it what you will—forms the whole sum and substance of the philosophy called 'Egoism,' and the man who, after due reflection, subscribes himself to it, becomes a 'Conscious Egoist;' conscious! mark you—in that alone lies the difference between himself and the unbeliever; for, according to his philosophy, all men are Egoists by an inevitable law—the Supreme Law of Nature!"

Carl Panzram was a killer through and through. The reason we know his name beyond his electrocution in 1930 is the palpable poison of his diary:

"In my life time I have murdered 21 human beings. I have committed thousands of burglaries, robberies Larcenys, arsons and last but not least I have committed sodomy on more than 1,000 male human beings. for all of these things I am not the least bit sorry. I have no conscience so that does not worry me. I don't believe in Man, God nor devil. I hate the whole damed human race including myself... These two experiences taught me several lessons. Lesson that I have never forgotten. I did not want to learn these lessons but I found out that it isn't what one wants in this world that one gets. Forse and might makes right. Perhaps things shouldn't be that way but thats the way they are. I learned to look with suspission and hatred on everybody. As the years went on that idea persisted in my mind above all others. I figured that if I was strong enough and clever enough to impose my will on others, I was right. I still believe that to this day. Another lesson I learned at that time was that there were a lot of very nice things in this world. Among them were Whisky and Sodomy. But it depended on who and how they were used. I have used plenty of both since then but I have received more pleasure off of them since; than I did those first times. Those were the days when I was learning the lessons that life teaches us all and they made me what I am today... This lesson I was taught by others. Might makes right."

Charles Fort wondered at wheels in the sky and at spooks but he himself had no wheels in his head nor spooks:

"I believe nothing. I have shut myself away from the rocks and wisdom of ages, and from the so-called great teachers of all time, and perhaps because of that isolation I am given to bizarre hospitalities. I shut the front door upon Christ and Einstein, and at the back door hold out a welcoming hand to little frogs and periwinkles. I believe nothing of my own that I have ever written. I cannot accept that the products of the mind are subject-matter for beliefs." (*Lo!*, 1931).

"I conceive of nothing, in religion, science, or philosophy, that is more than the proper thing to wear, for a while." (*Wild Talents*, 1932).

The 1940s saw the advent of Brother Theodore and his stand-up tragedy.

"My name, as you may have guessed, is Theodore. I come from

a strange stock. The members of my family were mostly epileptics, vegetarians, stutterers, triplets, nailbiters. But we've always been happy. I am what you call a controversial figure. People either hate me or they despise me. I'm a somebody in a century of nobodies."

Egoism, anarchism and communism all went to the early-1900's ball, but we know which wicked stepsister got to dance for the next half-century. We don't see much of egoism again until Ayn Rand's Objectivism (*The Fountainhead* 1943, *Atlas Shrugged* 1957, and so very etc.). Dame Rand had a decent egoist rookie season, what with her admiration of murderer William Edward Hickman ("Other people do not exist for him, and he does not see why they should. [He had] no regard whatsoever for all that society holds sacred, and with a conscious all his own. He has the true, innate psychology of a Superman. He can never realize and feel 'other people.'"), her "rational self-interest," her railing against self-destruction while being a chain-smoker, her insistence on loyalty while having affairs. Truth and consistency be damned, hoist the dollar flag! But having dislodged the great Catherine wheel of altruism from her head, she let it fill with sand to make a perfect impression of liberty. While Ayn Rand could have served Ayn Rand, Ayn Rand instead served Objectivism. How many more steps away from freedom then are those intellectual heir brains who splinter from her fossilized remains. It was a no-fault divorce, egoism and Objectivism. "Egoism, in the Objectivist interpretation, does not mean the policy of violating the rights, moral or political, of others in order to satisfy one's own needs or desires. It does not mean the policy of a brute, a con man or a beggar." So said Leonard Peikoff in the revealingly-named *Objectivism: The Philosophy of Ayn Rand*. *Le objectivism, ce moi.* Objectivism put the vocabulary of egoism back into circulation. But instead of the dead-end of egoism (all roads lead to ME), Objectivism is an endless journey into ever-tighter circles of servitude.

Rudy Ray Moore may have been quoting an unknown homeless man from 1960 when he performed his "Dolemite" skit, but the results are me-tastic. Thus Spoke Dolemite:

> "Why the day he was dropped from his mammy's ass, he slapped his pappy's face and said from now on, I'm running this place. Dolemite said, bitch I had a job in Africa kicking lions in the ass to stay in shape. I got run out of South America for fucking steers. I fucked the she-elephant until she broke down in tears. I've swimmed across muddy rivers and ain't never got wet. Mountains fell on me and I ain't dead yet. I rode across the ocean on the head of my dick, ate nine tons of cat shit and ain't never got sick."

Atlas may have shrugged, but Dolemite stuck his dick in the ground and turned the whole world around.

The market is a bunch of things that only sort-of work together. Capitalism and socialism definitely sound great on paper but the world hasn't seen them just yet. The world has seldom seen a man like Ernest Mann, either. In the 1960s Mann quit his job, sold or gave away his possessions, and strove mightily to never work for money again. Plenty of armchair economists will tell you how to spend other people's time and money, but Mann walked the noble path and did it himself for decades before he suggested anyone else might do the same. He published a newsletter called Little Free Press which was collected into two books titled *I Was Robot* and *Free*

I Got. There was a harmony between what he thought and how he lived and what he wrote. He owned no thing, and no thing owned him.

Every costumed character in the comics is a vigilante using their unique powers to remake the world in their image. Some are labeled heroes and some are labeled rogues, but under the mask they are all egoists. In 1967 Steve Ditko (creator of Spiderman, Dr. Strange and many other characters) invented Mr. A, whose morality was as unbending as it was out of sync with an altruistic world. *V for Vendetta* asked in 1982 if it was better to go with the devil you know or roll the dice to see if the vigilante is more nice. Batman double-crossed the line between savior and villain in Frank Miller's *The Dark Knight Returns* (1986). Alan Moore tipped his hat to Mr. A. with the character Rorschach in his 1986 comic *Watchmen*. In 1999 Warren Ellis wrote *The Authority*, in which a team of superheroes make the obvious move in a world gone mad by taking it over. *The Walking Dead* by Robert Kirkman has zombies in it, sure, but since the comic began in 2003 the real conflict has been that old familiar story of men with competing interests and limited resources and only as much morality as they need, not what they'd like.

Muhammad Ali invented himself in 1964, the same year he defeated Sonny Liston to earn the Heavyweight Champion belt. He is The Greatest!

> "I'm experienced now! I'm a professional! Jaw's been broke, been knocked down a couple times, I'm bad! Been choppin' trees! I done something new for this fight—I done wrassled with an alligator! That's right! I have wrassled with an alligator, I done tussled with a whale, I done handcuffed lightnin', throwed thunder in jail! That's bad! Only last week I murdered

a rock, injured a stone, hospitalized a brick! I'm so mean I make medicine sick! Bad! Fast! Last night I cut the light off in my bedroom, hit the switch and was in the bed before the room was dark! And you, all you chumps are going to bow when I come whuppin'!"

Anton LaVey published *The Satanic Bible* in 1969. The Satanic Bible touched on *Might is Right* in it's "Book of Satan" chapter. Elsewhere LaVey wrote: "Do not take that which does not belong to you unless it is a burden to the other person and he cries out to be relieved." Let's say altruist Anton was helping Redbeard by helping himself. Not that LaVey couldn't deliver the goods on his own: "The Satanist believes in complete gratification of his ego. Satanism, in fact, is the only religion which advocates the intensification or encouragement of the ego... Life is the one great indulgence; death the one great abstinence. To a person who is satisfied with his earthly existence, life is like a party; and no one likes to leave a good party." LaVey did put on a good party, and current Magister Peter Gilmore has done a fine job as well. It it perhaps eternally tempting to resolve the contradictions invoked in orchestrating an organization for individualists, but the Church of Satan has kept it's claw clean.

The Situationists served two masters, the individual and the masses, but even when they fell on their asses those pierrot put on a good show. "The freedom of one will be the freedom of all. A community which is not built on the demands of individuals and their dialectic can only reinforce the oppressive violence of power. The Other in whom I do not find myself is nothing but a thing, and altruism leads me to the love of things, to the love of my isolation." (Raoul Vaneigem,

The Revolution of Everyday Life 1967). "When we begin to demolish the prisons inside us and destroy the killers of super-ego lying in ambush, the ones outside will fall like the Bastille. You arrive at totality only by having no more doubts. I only am what I am by making myself so for my own pleasure. You are in such a hurry to explain me you want an autopsy. No one is more curious about me than I am. Perhaps your tender solicitude helps me to see more clearly, but I am the only person who can let light through the shadows." (Raoul Vaneigem, *The Book of Pleasures* 1979).

Tell an egoist what he can't do and you can be sure he'll give it a go. As the philosophy of the self, egoism has no empathy for the philosophy of the rest. Nevertheless, in 1974 the group For Ourselves! issued *The Right to Be Greedy*, a merging of egoism and communism. Until recently (ahem) this was the most detailed criticism of egoism from within.

"'Nothing is more to me than myself.' Fine. As it stands, this theorem is wholly acceptable. This is a classic statement of the egoistic postulate by the classic exponent of individualist anarchism and narrow egoism, and an early antagonist of Marx, Max Stirner. His latter-day followers, conscious and unconscious, include the 'Objectivists,' the 'classical liberals,' and the so-called 'libertarian right' in general. The problem is that, in the further elaboration of his own book, Stirner's own understanding of his own statement proved to be unequal to it. Stirner proved to be insensitive to what the concept of 'self'—in order to be adequate to reality—must entail; what must be its content, if it is expanded (i.e., developed) beyond the level of its self-contradiction—namely all of the other selves which inter-mutually 'constitute' or produce it; in short, society. This error in general must be attributed to undeveloped concrete self-knowledge; Stirner did not know himself, his own true identity. He did not know himself as society, or society as his real self."

Loompanics Unlimited was founded in 1975. Until founder Michael Hoy closed shop in 2006, Loompanics published and distributed after the egoist fashion. Far left? Far right? Humor? Sex? Drugs? Parapsychology? And even some straight-up egoist titles and authors such as those honored here? Loompanics had it all, just no gods and no masters. In 2013 I can read most anything I like on a computer I carry in My pocket. In decades past, more ideas still had the stink of heresy on them and finding them in a book mattered. *The Myth of Natural Rights* and *Lucifer's Lexicon* were first published by Loompanics in the 1980s. Loompanics was the last egoist monster movie shot on film before everything went digital. Most important of all, it was through Loompanics that egoism had the privilege of meeting Me.

While egoism is bookish there are veins of egoism throbbing in other media. The song Big Rock Candy Mountain by Harry McClintock describes a paradise where they hung the jerk that invented work. Some of the songs of the Great Depression had men of no apparent means declaring themselves master of all they surveyed. Punk was many things, among them a solid shove to society to make room for the irksome individual. Like all youth cultures it got old, but the anger is preserved in amber. At nearly the same time, The Residents and Devo and Laibach provided three different counterpoints to individualism in music. In the 1980s Boyd Rice gave us *Music, Martinis and Misanthropy* which quoted from *Might is Right* while N.W.A. gave us Straight Outta Compton with Eazy E as a one man Bonnot gang. It's the bullet or the ballad! Whitehouse began performing their sonic assaults on their audience in 1982. One more song ("Love's Secret Domain" by Coil, from 1991) then on to the visual arts. The 1966 program *The Prisoner* is the premier example of man against men and men against man from the medium of television. *Cool Hand Luke* (1967) and *Harold and Maude* (1971) are films for individualists. *Paradise Now* by the Living Theatre (1968) is a play in harmony with a union of egoists. The 14 October 2001 episode of the television program *Aqua Teen Hunger Force*, "Mayhem of the Mooninites," includes egoist characters.

Praise "Bob"! The Church of the SubGenius commemorates its founding on January 1, 1980, the day Pamphlet Number One arrived from the printers. In SubGenius doctrine the world will end on July 5th, 1998 when angelic UFOs shepherd paid members to Planet X, while the unsaved writhe on a hellish Earth now lacking the founder of the Church, J. R. "Bob" Dobbs. Since conventional calendars tell us July 5th 1998 has come and gone, there must be something wrong with time itself. From *The Brag of the SubGenius*:

> "I speak only the fucking Truth, and never in my days have I spoken other than! For my every utterance is a lie, including this very one you hear! I say, 'Fuck'em if they can't take a joke!' By God, 'Anything for a laugh,' I say. I am the last remaining Homo Correctus, I am the god damn Man of the Future! I'll drive a mile so as not to walk a foot; I am a human being of the first god-damn water! Yes, I'm the javalina-humping junkie that jumped the Men from Mars! I drank the Devil under seven tables, I am too intense to die, I'm insured for acts o' God and Satan!"

Thee Temple ov Psychick Youth touched on the self in their 1981 founding document, *Thee Grey Book*:

"Clean out the trappings and debris of compromise, of what you've been told is reasonable for a person in your circumstances. Be clear in admitting your real desires. Discard all irrelevancies. Ask yourself who you want as friends, it you need or want to work, what you want to eat. Check and re-check everything deeper and deeper, more and more precisely to get closer to and ultimately integrate with yourself. Once you are focused on your Self internally, the external aspects of your life will fall into place."

Search and Destroy Magazine and its second life *Re/Search Magazine* have long investigated the control process and how an individual might break free. Just before their *Modern Primitives* issue broke into the mainstream came Re/Search 11, *Pranks!* in 1986. It would be an own goal to imitate any particular prank or prankster, but the pranks issue of *Re/Search* is a fine compilation of how black a black sheep can be. There is an underground river flowing from the Suicide Club to the Cacophony Society to *Pranks!* to *Fight Club* by Chuck Palahniuk to *Jackass* by Johnny Knoxville. Hop in, the water is dangerous!

Queer had a spark of life in it for a heartbeat in the 1990s. For a brief time sex was what an individual said it was, independent of labels or expectation. What was an infinite number of shades in the rainbow were muted to just a few. It wasn't AIDS that cooled the heat, it was that choking vine called community. There's a place for you to march, march, march in the pride parade. Go AWOL! You can still make out the musk of liberty in free love.

Your humble author had the privilege of publishing essays by Hakim Bey before they were compiled in his 1991 book *T. A. Z. The Temporary Autonomous Zone*. *T. A. Z.* matters to egoism because it points out how little I need a cause or a group or a place or even time to carve out some measure of individual liberty. "Don't just survive while waiting for someone's revolution to clear your head, don't sign up for the armies of anorexia or bulimia—act as if you were already free, calculate the odds, step out, remember the Code Duello—Smoke Pot/Eat Chicken/Drink Tea. Every man his own vine & figtree (Circle Seven Koran, Noble Drew Ali)—carry your Moorish passport with pride, don't get caught in the crossfire, keep your back covered—but take the risk, dance before you calcify." An aside: *T. A. Z.* references an earlier (1983), lesser-known but recommended book called *bolo'bolo* by P. M.

Boyd Rice turned his talents to text in the 2009 book *NO*. "All modern thought is predicated upon belief in the unbelievable... I mistrust every ideal cherished in western democratic civilization. The words that make others smile and nod in agreement cause me to recoil. Insofar as I can figure, I seem to have been born a sociopath of sorts." Yes you can say no!

You like a laugh, right? Check this out: "everyone should do what they want as long as they don't hurt anybody else." Now there's a genuine knee-slapper! When boots are on the ground (or the back of your neck) it turns out there aren't enough resources or time such that that we can all do as we want without hurting anybody else. The symphony of the spheres is more like musical chairs, and when the music stops somebody didn't get what they wanted at all. Not at all. One of the few books of practical philosophy is *The Way of Men* by Jack Donovan, published in 2012.

> "When you ask men about what makes a real man, a lot of them will get up on their high horses and start talking about what it means to be a good man. [...] There is a difference between being a good man and being good at being a man. [...] Being good at being a man is about being willing and able to fulfill the natural role of men in a survival scenario. Being good at being a man is about showing other men that you are the kind of guy they'd want on their team if the shit hits the fan. Being good at being a man isn't a quest for moral perfection, it's about fighting to survive. Good men admire or respect bad men when they demonstrate strength, courage, mastery or a commitment to the men of their own renegade tribes. A concern with being good at being a man is what good guys and bad guys have in common."

The vagabond Apio Ludd works hard for being such a bum. He taught himself German to do original translations of Stirner, then he taught himself Italian to do original translations of Novatore. If you are exceptionally fortunate you'll meet Ludd as he rolls through town, and you just might be able to get a copy of his zine *My Own* (January 2012—eternity). "I strive in each moment to create my life as my own. This is a life project, a project with no final goal and no end other than my own... I am not trying to start a movement or gain adherents for a cause. This would itself promote a form of enslavement that may perhaps be radically different, but that would still interfere with my self-creating and which would make me the tool of some imagined 'higher power,' the cause to which I have enchained myself—a thing that doesn't interest me in the least."

Terminus! BEHOLD! An egoist inoculation by the mithridatic method: *Confessions of a Failed Egoist* by Trevor Blake. Full disclosure, that's Me! I am an egoist, a circular thinker of the most self-contained philosophy...

WM. TREVOR BLAKE

Born May 1, 1966 Knoxville, Tennessee USA.
Since 1992, living in Portland, Oregon USA.
Publisher of OVO magazine, 1987–present.
Online publisher, 1991–present.

BOOKS BY TREVOR BLAKE:

Confessions of a Failed Egoist by Trevor Blake. Baltimore,
    Underworld Amusements 2014.
Portland Memorials by Trevor Blake. Portland, OVO 2011.

BOOKS INCLUDING WORK
BY TREVOR BLAKE:

The SubGenius Psychlopaedia of Slack by Ivan Stang. New
    York, Thunder's Mouth Press 2006.
The Journal of Ride Theory Omnibus by Dan Howland.
    Portland, JORT 2003.
Strange Creations by Donna Kossy. Los Angeles, Feral
    House 2001.
Revelation X by Ivan Stang. New York, Simon & Schuster 1994.
Kooks by Donna Kossy. Portland, Feral House 1994.
In Extremis by Bill Babouris. Athens Greece, Survival
    Kit 1994.
Killing for Culture by David Kerekes. London, Creation
    Books 1994.
Anarchy and the End of History by Mike Gunderloy. New
    York, Factsheet Five 1991.
Killer Fiction by Sondra London. Atlanta, Media Queen 1991.

Three-Fisted Tales of "Bob" by Ivan Stang. New York, Simon & Schuster 1990.

semiotext(e) USA by Jim Flemming and Peter Wilson. New York, Autonomedia 1987.

Pozdravi iz Babilona by KRT. Ljubljana, KRT 1987.

BOOKS INCLUDING TREVOR BLAKE:

Undercover Mormon by Th. Metzger. New York, Roadswell Editions 2014.

The Way of Men by Jack Donovan. Portland, Dissonant Hum 2012.

Blood Brotherhood by Jack Donovan and Nathan Miller. Portland, Dissonant Hum 2009.

Akashic Record of the Astral Convention by Hakim Bey. Portland, EsoZone 2007.

'Zine by Pagan Kennedy. New York, St. Martin's Press 1995.

The World of Zines by Mike Gunderloy. New York, Penguin Books 1992.

T.A.Z. The Temporary Autonomous Zone by Hakim Bey. New York, Autonomedia 1991.

Loompanics Greatest Hits by Michael Hoy. Port Townsend, Loompanics 1990.

High Weirdness by Mail by Ivan Stang. New York, Simon & Schuster 1988.

TREVOR BLAKE
P. O. BOX 2321
PORTLAND. OR 97208-2321
USA

Other titles you may enjoy from

UNDERWORLD AMUSEMENTS
WWW.UNDERWORLDAMUSEMENTS.COM

Homo, 99 and 44/100%
Nonsapeins
Revised with a new Introduction
by Gerald B. Lorentz
6x9, 424 pages, $18.95

A Bible Not Borrowed
from the Neighbors.
Essays and Aphorisms on Egoism
Edited by Kevin I. Slaughter
6x9, 164 pages, $14.95

Men versus the Man
Socialism versus Individualism
by H.L. Mencken and Robert
Rives La Monte
Preface by John Derbyshire
6x9, 204 pages, $15.95

The Sorceries and
Scandals of Satan
by Henry M. Tichenor
foreword by R. Merciless
6x9, 176 pages, $15.95

ANATHEMA!
Litanies of Negation
by Benjamin DeCasseres
Foreword by Eugene O'Neill
Afterword by Kevin I. Slaughter
6x9, 66 pages, $9.99

IMP
The Poetry of Benjamin DeCasseres
by Benjamin DeCasseres
Introduction by Kevin I. Slaughter
6x9, 196 pages, $14.95

Made in the USA
Lexington, KY
04 April 2014